Electric Guitar Handbook

Electric Guitar Handbook

Richard Riley

PC Publishing

PC Publishing
Export House
130 Vale Road
Kent TN9 1SP
UK

Tel 01732 770893
Fax 01732 770268
email info@pc-pubs.demon.co.uk
website http://www.pc-pubs.demon.co.uk

First published 1998

ISBN 1 870775 47 3

British Library Cataloguing in Publication Data
A catalogue record for this book is available from the British Library

Printed in Great Britain by Bell and Bain, Glasgow

Preface

In 1977 with my friend Andy Faulkener I had a guitar lesson in a little teaching studio above our local guitar store. We went together because neither of us knew how to play, Andy was heavily into Elvis Presley, I went along to back him up. So we sat in a room with five other people, each of us had a little headphone amp and some music. My problem is that I'm a little impatient so reading music (the dots and lines) always came after the fun part for me. Instead of learning how to play the chord that our instructor was showing us I got distracted by the pickup selector switch on the guitar. I knew that switch did something but I didn't know why. Worse, I could hear that it was doing something to the sound but what and how? Even worse it bugged me to hell. I mean why have a switch that did nothing? Was there another switch I had to pull first? I went home and took my guitar apart to find out and in the process of putting it back together again I discovered just how neat this construction of wood, metal and wire could be.

Now I've played, made, repaired, messed with and messed up, written about and loved guitars for as long as I can remember. I have also been fortunate enough to make a living from being associated with guitars in many ways. I'll never forget my first guitar lesson, I knew then that it was the start of a long journey and twenty years later I'm still learning. If you are just starting out I hope you will find some answers here. Just one thing; if there's a moral to all this, it's probably that the more sure you are about the answer, the more likely you are to be wrong. But this book is a darn good place to start.

This book is for anyone who needs to know – without knowing why.

'All my life, I've spent the nights with dreams of you ...'
Disney Girls – The Beach Boys

Dedication

For Smiles
And my Dad.

Contents

Acknowledgements

This book wouldn't have been possible without the generous help and assistance of these people and many others too numerous to mention. Akai UK, Andie Brooke-Mellor at FCN, Audrey Riley, Ben at Rosetti, Charlie Stringers Snarlin' Dogs!, Darren Power of Yamaha UK, Dave Burrluck for 'Thunderbolt' and Music Industry statistics, Frosa at Korg UK, Ian Miller, James York of the V&A for time and history, Joe Bennett for the old Yamaha, Jo Riley and Chip, John and Julie Emery, Larry DiMarzio, Lloyd Gilbert, Louise at Peavey, Martyn Booth, Michael Leonard of The Guitar Magazine for Brit Builder listings, Nick and Liz Matthews, Nick Sharples at Arbiter, Phil Chapman at PC Publishing, Photo Permissions, Roger Meyer of Meyer effects, Roland/Boss UK, Simon Fraser Clarke for Ibanez material, Simon Turnbull at John Hornby Skewes, Simon Young for Future Guitar tips, Terrorvision, The Guitar Magazine, Tim Tucker, Tom Wheeler (*The Guitar Book*), Tony Horkins, Total Guitar, Walter Carter of Gibson USA for photo permissions and Gibson history.

Special thanks to Matt McArdle for photography in Chapters 7, 8 and 12.

Lace Sensor is a registered trademark of Actodyne General Incorporated. *DiMarzio and PAF* are some of the registered trademarks of DiMarzio Inc. *Fender, Esquire, Stratocaster, Telecaster, Broadcaster, Jaguar, Strat, Tele* and *Squier* are some of the registered trademarks of Fender Musical Instruments Inc. *Gibson, Les Paul, SG, Flying V, ES-335* and *Tune-O-Matic* are some of the registered trademarks of the Gibson Guitar Corp. All other registered trademarks are acknowledged.

The electric guitar

Who invented the electric guitar? Many people. It's known that during the early 1900's inventors were experimenting with guitar pickups from phonograph parts. Perhaps Lloyd Loar with his early experiments with microphones is the true inventor of the electric guitar. Perhaps George Beauchamp for the single coil pickup, or Paul Bigsby for the contoured body.

This book is about modern electric guitars – guitars which are still around (and played, and made) today. For most people this begins with the Fender Broadcaster in 1949 and the Gibson Les Paul in 1952.

The electric guitar

The electric guitar is a musical instrument with six or twelve metal strings stretched over a wooden body. Typically the body and neck are of wood with other parts of chrome finished steel or brass. The guitar is a plucked instrument, although other methods of playing, such as tapping and bowing, are practised. The vibration of the strings causes the pickups to produce small amounts of electrical current which are amplified by external equipment connected to the guitar.

Lloyd Loar – inventor of the electric guitar? (Copyright and courtesy of Gibson Guitar Corp)

The electric guitar is cheap to produce, easily learnt and great fun to play. Above all the electric guitar is noted for its unique ability to inspire feelings of joy, transcendental awareness and satisfaction in the player. Awe, inspiration, lust ... and the need to buy records ... in the listener.

Fair enough, with a few buts ...

Guitar bodies are not always made of wood. Electric guitars have been made of metal, stone, plastic, epoxy resin, carbon graphite and any combination of the above. Steinberg guitars have high technology moulded bodies with wooden tops for looks and strength.

Most guitars have six strings. Bass guitars have four. The outrageous Hamer B12A Electric Bass has 12 strings in four courses (sets) of three strings. Electric and acoustic guitars might have six, ten or twelve strings.

Electric guitars can have three or four necks! Rick Nielsen has a five-neck guitar made by Hamer. Some guitars have two necks, one bass and one regular or one six and one twelve. Guitarist Michael Angelo has a twin

✦ INFO ✦

If you want to know more about the history of the electric guitar, there is a very useful list of reference material at the end of this book.

neck guitar set like a mirror; one neck pointing left and one pointing right! Some electric guitars don't even need to be connected to an amp.

Child make 3/4 size guitars both with a small 1 watt amp inside, so do Pignose. The first Sears and Roebuck electric guitars arrived with a small tube amp built into the case! An electro-acoustic guitar is an acoustic guitar with an electric pickup somewhere in the body, usually underneath the bridge. This kind of guitar can be used without an amplifier (acoustically) or with an amplifier (electrically) Like a convertible car. The point is:

The best thing about the guitar is that as soon as you make a rule — somebody will break it !

Solid bodied electric guitars

A solid bodied electric guitar has a solid body with small cavities to house pickups and electronics. By definition, an electric guitar is a guitar without an internal chamber for vibrating air but with a pickup (or microphone) for converting string vibrations or sound waves into electrical pulses which may be amplified and turned back into sound waves via a speaker. So any guitar with a pickup might be called an 'electric guitar'. It's confusing.

Usually guitars are referred to by their model name or manufacturer's name. So you might go into a store and say 'Can I see a Stratocaster?' Right away the salesperson knows what you want and isn't going to bring out a nylon string classical with a Fishman pickup.

Terms like 'lead guitar' or 'axe' now thankfully seem to be redundant. A Gibson Les Paul is a solid bodied guitar, so is a Jackson JJ1, a Fender Duo-Sonic, an Epiphone Les Paul, a Paul Reed Smith and an Encore Vintage. The list goes on and on.

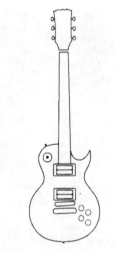

Outline of a typical solid bodied guitar

Semi-solid guitars

A semi-solid guitar has a solid body with two hollow wings. The 'semi-acoustic' term is a corruption of the correct 'semi-solid' name given to guitars with this construction. Crucially some solid guitars also have hollow sides but the top must feature an 'f' hole to be known as a semi-solid. Although these guitars can be used without an amplifier they are much quieter than a regular acoustic guitar.

Examples of semi-solid guitars include Epiphone 'The Dot', Gibson 335, Fender Thinline, Rickenbacker 360, Gretsch White Falcon and many others. The development of the 'semi' goes right back to Les Paul and his prototype solid bodied guitar which he built in Epi Stathopoulo's (Epiphone) workshop in 1941. His Les Paul was a solid log between two halves of a jazz guitar.

Semi-solid guitars have similar properties to solid guitars except that the larger volume of moving air inside the instrument gives the electric sound of the guitar a deeper, richer quality. The larger volume of moving air also makes semi-solid guitars more susceptible to feedback.

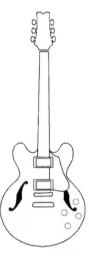

Outline of a semi-solid guitar

Other types

Semi-hollow guitars
Some 'solid' guitars have hollow bodies, or large cavities but without 'f' holes. These are called semi-hollow. This design takes advantage of the enhanced bass of a semi-solid guitar but the absence of 'f' holes reduces the guitar's susceptibility to feedback.

Most manufacturers now make a semi-hollow guitar including Gretsch with their Malcolm Young signature model, the Brian Moore MC/1 and Gibson's Custom Shop, who claim their modern semi-hollow Les Paul guitars emulate the sound of the mahogany used during the 1950's without the expense or the environmental impact.

Arch top guitars
Arch top or carved top guitars are large bodied electric guitars with a traditional braced construction. They feature large hollow bodies, cutaways at the 12th fret and 'f' holes. Pickups can either be mounted onto the guitar top or attached to the very end of the neck above the body. Jazz players choose guitars like these for their deep resonant sound and full acoustic projection. Examples include Fender D'Aquisto Ultra, Ibanez GB10, Epiphone Broadway.

Acoustic guitars
An acoustic guitar needs no external amplification as vibrations from the guitar bridge cause the air inside the body to vibrate. Variations on acoustic guitars are as numerous as they are for electric guitars.

If an acoustic guitar has a pickup it is often concealed within the bridge of the guitar. Small piezo crystals are hidden in the bridge and connected to an amplifier by a jack socket hidden on the underside of the guitar or within the strap button. Because piezo pickups produce very small amounts of electricity the output needs to be boosted by a pre-amp system mounted either in the guitar body or outside in the form of a foot pedal. An additional advantage of having a pre-amp is the extra control it allows over the tone and volume of the guitar. Acoustic guitars are much more susceptible to feedback, and the additional tone control enables the experienced player to minimise this risk without interrupting the performance.

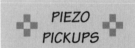

PIEZO PICKUPS

A piezo pickup uses the natural ability of some minerals to produce small voltages if vibrated or subjected to mechanical pressure. Because the crystal is very small the pickup may be hidden inside the bridge of the guitar without detracting from the guitar's appearance.

An A to Z of the guitar

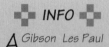

Vintage non-tremolo bridge for solid guitar

Binding

Binding is a decorative effect applied to the guitar during manufacture. It is used to highlight the edges of the guitar by drawing a line around the outside edge. The binding is always in a contrasting colour and can be wood, plastic or any material which can be shaped and glued to the body before the finish is applied..

Body

The body of the guitar begins at the lowest point (usually where the strap button at the bottom of the guitar is fixed) and extends to where the neck of the guitar leaves the body (the heel).

The guitar body can be made of almost any material and can be any shape, but because the amplified sound of the electric guitar is affected by body shape and weight, the shape of the electric guitar must be carefully designed to produce the best sound possible within the limits dictated by weight, size and cost of materials. The dimensions of a typical electric guitar body would be 400mm by 350mm. The thickness of the guitar body depends on the model and materials.

Bridge

The bridge of the guitar is one of only two places where the guitar string meets the body (the other is the nut). The function of the bridge is to hold the string above the fingerboard and body and to stop the string at a crucial distance away from the nut to enable the guitar to play in tune. This distance from the nut to the bridge is called the 'scale'.

Bridge pieces or saddles

Because an important part of playing the guitar is using the high frets above the twelvth, where intonation and action are crucial, the guitar has individual bridge pieces for each string. This allows fine adjustment of intonation and string height so the guitar remains in tune even at the higher frets.

Control cavities

Control cavities contain the pickups and other electronic components that the manufacturer installs. Cavities are routed out of the guitar before the finish is applied. Too many cavities are bad for your guitar as air can vibrate in the cavities which affects the sound produced by the solid body. Sometimes thin plastic covers are screwed over the cavities to protect the electronics.

Controls
These allow the player to control the volume and tone of the guitar. Small switches are used for advanced pickup functions, such as phase reversal, coil drop and coil tap. Guitars can also have switches for another pickup system, any special effects built into the guitar, and MIDI functions.

Cutaway
The cutaway enables the guitar player to reach right over the body of the guitar when playing at the high upper frets. Some acoustic guitars also have a cutaway.

Fingerboard
The fingerboard lies on top of the neck and is usually a separate piece of wood which is glued onto the neck during manufacture. Fingerboards are normally made of a decorative hard wood such as maple or rosewood. Depending on the manufacturer and the availability of materials, an expensive hand made guitar might have an ebony fingerboard. Frets are laid into slots in the fingerboard which is shaped to have a slight curve. This curve is called the radius.

Fender Telecaster® has pickup selector, volume and tone controls

F hole
Semi-acoustic guitars have large air cavities inside the guitar. The F hole allows the top to vibrate so the guitar can be acoustically louder.

Finish
The guitar's finish is very important as it is often a key factor in the instrument's appeal to the potential buyer. It is usually a combination of gloss, colour and decoration. Guitars can be finished in a solid colour, a graduated colour called a 'sunburst' or a transparent colour which allows some of the detail in the wood to show. Some guitars are left uncoloured to let the wood's natural pattern show through. These are normally finished in cellulose lacquer, polyurethane varnish, or even oil or wax.

Fret markers
Fret markers or position dots show the player where the third, fifth, ninth, twelfth, fifteenth, seventeenth, nineteenth, twenty first and twenty fourth frets are!

Frets
Frets stop the string when the player presses down on the string just behind the fret. This enables a clear note to sound. Frets are made from nickel–silver alloy.

Fret markers help you find your way around

Fender Stratocaster® jack socket (above) and machine heads (below)

Roland GK2A MIDI pickup

Headstock

The headstock provides a flat surface to which the machine heads or tuners are fitted. As the most visual part of the guitar the headstock is used by the maker to signal what kind of guitar it is, who the maker is and even what kind of music might be played on this guitar. To an experienced player one glance at the headstock can often say more than words ever can, even at a distance.

Heel

The heel is the point where the neck of the guitar joins the body.

Inlay

Decorative inlay is used along the neck, and sometimes elsewhere on the guitar to add value by making the guitar more complex and difficult to copy. Most manufacturers offer at least one model with lots of decoration. The inlay is usually cut from very thin sheets of mother of pearl and glued into place.

Jack socket

The jack socket is used to connect the guitar to an amplifier. The guitar cord or lead connects to this socket and into an identical socket at the amplifier. It doesn't matter which end of the cord plugs into which. The jack socket is a 1/4 inch mono phone socket. Stereo phone sockets are often used on guitars with complex switching and pickup combinations.

Machine heads

Tuning pegs are called machine heads because they use a high gearing ratio (usually 12 or 15:1) to enable the player to slowly rotate the tuning peg and bring the guitar exactly to pitch. Twelve turns of the head are required to rotate the peg one full turn.

MIDI pickup

A MIDI pickup fitted to the guitar allows the guitarist to control MIDI equipment. In this case the guitar sound itself is immaterial as the MIDI equipment is emulating the sound of the guitar. Some systems enable the player to mix the actual sound of the guitar with the synthesised sound for additional realism.

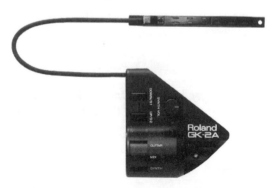

Neck

The neck of the guitar supports the fingerboard and acts as a bed for the truss rod to lie in. The neck is shaped to feel comfortable to the player. Different guitar designs have different neck 'profiles'. A solid bodied electric guitar may have a bolt on or a set neck. A set neck means that the neck is glued and jointed to the guitar body and cannot be adjusted. A bolt on neck can be adjusted or even replaced but the sound of the guitar is diminished.

Fender guitars have a thick V shaped neck. Gibson and other guitars have a flatter, wider C shape.

Five way pickup selector switch

Nut

The guitar nut holds the strings above the fingerboard and provides a stop for an open string. Grooves in the nut maintain the string spacing.

Pickup

A pickup senses string vibrations and transmits them as electrical impulses to an amplifier or effects unit. Humbucking pickups are generally louder than single coil pickups. Single coil pickups are usually clearer and brighter than humbucking pickups.

Pickup selector switch

A guitar with more than one pickup is often fitted with a pickup selector switch to enable the player to choose just one or all of the pickups, depending on the guitar and the pickup configuration. Pushing the switch up selects the neck or 'rhythm' pickup. Pushing the switch down selects the bridge or 'lead' pickup.

Different models have different selector switches, some enable the user to select a combination of pickups. Les Paul guitars have a three way switch enabling the rhythm, rhythm and lead or just the lead pickup to be activated.

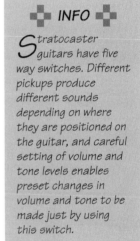

Purfling

This is an ornamental or decorative strip inlaid into the top of the guitar just behind the binding strip and around the sound hole on an acoustic guitar. The strip is filled with a wooden strip of contrasting colour, mother-of-pearl or abalone.

Scratches and dents

Scratches are an inevitable part of an guitars life. Most minor scratches can be ignored as they have no ill effects on the guitar or its sound. Deep scratches and cracks need attention as the guitar must remain strong to cope with high string pressure (and lively use!).

Chipped and peeling paint, tarnished metalwork even rust is now considered to be a positive virtue – meaning the guitar has had a long and full life and therefore is likely to be valuable!

Decorative scratchplate on
Fender Telecaster®

Scratchplate

The scratchplate was invented for Spanish Flamenco guitars to prevent the fingernails of the guitarist tearing premature holes in the guitar top! As guitar finishes became more valuable the scratchplate began to appear on acoustic guitars as a small piece of tortoiseshell just under the sound-hole. Fender and other electric guitar manufacturers mount pickups and fittings directly into the scratchplate.

'Skunk' stripe

Typically, Leo Fender was always looking for a more efficient way to put his guitars together. While other manufacturers were using a piece of wood for the neck, laying the truss rod in and gluing a fingerboard on top, Leo invented a procedure whereby the neck and fingerboard were made from one piece of maple. The truss rod was laid in a channel at the rear of the neck and the channel was finished with a piece of contrasting wood. This is the skunk stripe.

Strap button

Without which you would not be able to hang your guitar from a strap. Locking strap buttons stop the strap falling off.

String guides

String guides on the headstock keep the string as straight as possible between machine head and nut. This is important for tuning stability and aids sustain.

Sustain

The amount of time that a string will vibrate for after being struck or pulled. A long sustain is important if you play long flowing passages.

Tailpiece

The tailpiece anchors the string below the bridge on a Les Paul and other guitars with a separate bridge and tailpiece design. Most Fender guitars have a combination bridge and tailpiece. The tailpiece can be almost any-where behind the bridge as the string has already been stopped at the bridge, but it needs to be a firm anchor to enhance sustain and tuning sta-bility.

Tremolo arm

The tremolo arm is a lever that is used to force the bridge up and away from the guitar against the pull of springs at the rear. As the bridge comes up the strings slacken causing the pitch to drop. The important thing to remember is that this can happen while the string is vibrating so allowing a smooth lowering in pitch as long as the arm is depressed. When the arm is released, springs pull the bridge back to its original posi-tion onto the top of the guitar.

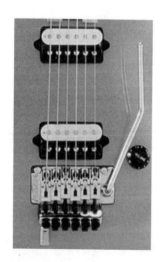

Tremolo arm on the Peavey
Wolfgang Vintage

Tremolo springs
Tremolo springs are attached to the bottom of the tremolo bridge and the guitar body. They are under tension all the time but more so when the tremolo arm is depressed.

Top
The body of the guitar is often capped with another thinner piece of dense wood such as alder or spruce, which adds to the decorative finish of the guitar while producing a brighter tone. Highly figured maple tops are prized amongst players who often value the look of a '10 Top' over the sound (maple is graded according to figuring by the manufacturer, higher grades are kept back for handmade and custom instruments). The figuring is produced by the dense grain of the wood. Les Paul guitars have always been made with a maple top over a mahogany body.

Truss rod cover
A plate covering the cavity through which the adjustable nut for the truss rod can be accessed.

Veloute
Some guitars are famous for having a weak point where the neck meets the headstock. The veloute is a an area of wood which isn't carved as thin as the headstock or neck which provides a strong point at the rear of the headstock just behind the nut.

3

Strings and things

Without the simplest motion – that of a vibrating string – the guitar would be nothing more than a good looking paperweight.

The principle of a vibrating string

The guitar string is held at tension between two points. One of the points is called the bridge, the other nearest the headstock is the nut. It is the job of the bridge to transfer vibrations from the string to the top of the guitar where they are amplified by the wooden top of the guitar. The bridge also provides support for the string to hold it above the top while dictating the precise point at which the string will stop vibrating. An electric guitar bridge has a slightly different function, it provides the string length but only some of the sound comes from body vibrations. Most of the sound of the electric guitar is generated by the pickups reacting to the string rather than the sound of the moving air created by the string vibrations. When any string suspended like this is hit, plucked or strummed it vibrates in a figure of eight pattern between the two anchor points. When a picked open string vibrates along its entire length the note is called the fundamental. If a harmonic is played at the twelfth fret each half of the string will vibrate at twice the frequency of the open string. This is called the second harmonic. This and others are summed up in the table.

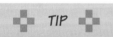

To play a harmonic lightly damp the low E string at the 12th fret and pick the string with a plectrum. As you hit the string immediately remove your left hand, the art is to lift the finger just as you feel the string vibrate. It's tricky but with practice you'll hear the harmonic note ring out.

Harmonics

Fret number	Number of harmonic
Fret 12	second harmonic
Fret 7	third harmonic
Fret 5	fourth harmonic
Fret 9	fifth harmonic

Two factors are critical if the guitar is to play in tune; tension (based on diameter) and length. Tension is provided by the tuning machines or 'tuners' which keep the string at a constant tension. String length is dictated and stabilised by the bridge which must be finely adjustable if the guitar is to have good intonation. If these two factors are in tune then the guitar will play in tune. If one is out then the guitar will never be in tune.

Tuning

Each string of the guitar must be tuned to vibrate at a standard frequency if the guitar is to be played in tune with other musicians.

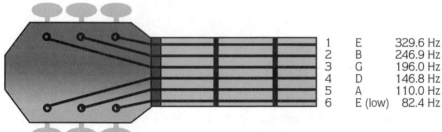

1	E	329.6 Hz
2	B	246.9 Hz
3	G	196.0 Hz
4	D	146.8 Hz
5	A	110.0 Hz
6	E (low)	82.4 Hz

Guitar strings and frequencies

When tuning to a piano use the A that is one octave below the A below Middle C as your reference. If using a tuning fork tune two octaves below an 'A' 440Hz tuning fork.

Guitar tuning to a piano keyboard

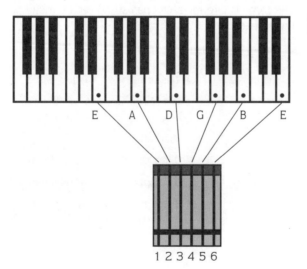

E   A   D   G   B   E

1 2 3 4 5 6

Electronic guitar tuners

For most people an electronic guitar tuner is the easiest and most convenient aid to tuning. The guitar is plugged into the tuner and the tuner detects which note you are playing. Then the tuner compares the frequency of your note with its own table of frequencies to decide whether your guitar is sharp or flat. Sharp means the guitar has to be tuned down, flat means the string has to be tightened.

There are different types of tuners, most have lights or a dial which swings right when your note is sharp, left when flat. When the dial or LED is centred, or both are on, the guitar string is in tune.

When choosing a tuner try and find a 'chromatic' model. A good exam-

Electronic guitar tuner. This string is flat!

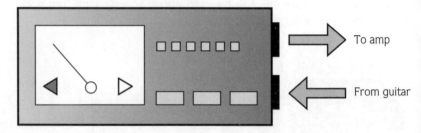

To amp

From guitar

ple is the Boss TU12 or TU12B for bass. This type of tuner is able to recognise which note you are playing. Non chromatic tuners need to be told which string you wish to tune before it can tell whether or not you are right or wrong. This can get a bit boring as you'll need to swap notes six times to tune the whole guitar. Pitchpipes and tuning forks can also be used as an aid to tuning, usually to provide a starting point from where the other strings can be tuned.

Tuning the guitar with fretted and open strings

The correct note for each open string can be found at this position on the fingerboard.

Tuning the guitar by fretting

Fret this note	On this string	Tune this string
Fret 5	6 (bottom E string)	5 (A string)
Fret 5	5 (A string)	4 (D string)
Fret 5	4 (D String)	3 (G string)
Fret 4	3 (G string)	2 (B string)
Fret 5	2 (B string)	1 (top E String)

An alternative method of tuning:

This note	And this note	Are both an
Open 6th (bottom E string)	String 5, Fret 7	E note
Open 5th (A string)	String 4, Fret 7	A note
Open 4th (D string)	String 3, Fret 7	D note
Open 3rd (G string)	String 2, Fret 8	G note
Open 2nd (B string)	String 1, Fret 7	B note
Open 1st (top E string)	String 5, Fret 7	E note

Both these methods of tuning rely on the low E string having already been checked with a tuning fork or pitch-pipe. To ensure that the whole guitar doesn't creep slowly out of tune as you work along the strings, periodically play a high E harmonic (fret 12, 1st string) and compare it with the same harmonic played on the low E string (fret 5, string 6)

Tuning with harmonics

Harmonics notes played at these positions will sound in unison. i.e. the same note will be heard. This procedure is very useful for comparing the tuning of two open strings as the pure sound waves produced by each harmonic cancel each other out causing the player to hear 'beats'. Experienced guitarists use this method to tune the strings in sympathy. As the strings become tuned to each other the beats gradually get faster until no beats are heard at all.

Tuning with harmonics

Tune harmonic at this position	To harmonic at this position
Fret 7 A string	Fret 5, Low E string
Fret 7 D string	Fret 5, A string
Fret 7 G string	Fret 5, D string
Fret 7 High E string	Fret 5, B string

NB The harmonic at fret 7 on the B string will not sound in unison with a harmonic played at fret 5 on the G string

All this is important because most people can hear if a musical instrument is in tune or not – even if they don't play themselves. Putting your guitar in tune before you play is a very worthwhile habit to get into.

Action and scale

'I don't want no satisfaction, all I want is easy action baby ...' Marc Bolan.

For many years I believed that Marc Bolan was singing about his poorly set up guitar. Little did I know that he had more earthly matters on his mind. But I was right in a way.

The action of your guitar is the distance between the frets and the bottom of the string, usually measured in thousands of an inch. It's this distance – literally how far the string must travel before being stopped by the fret – that many people judge to be the definition of a particularly good or poor setup, and consequently a good or bad guitar. For most players it's a case of 'the closer the action, the better the axe' and a low action is often quoted as a guitar selling point.

Do you ever get confused when you hear other players talking about guitars in terms of 'That's a great guitar – really low action!'? It's as if an action was something else you could buy to make the guitar sound better, or the more expensive a guitar is – the better the action. None of this is true. You either love or hate the way your guitar feels to you and this 'playability' is a combination of three factors, two immovable and one adjustable.

'Scale' and 'radius' are built into your guitar, and aren't adjustable. Action is dictated by two variables; string height and neck relief (plus a well set nut). All these ingredients add up to the character of that instrument. For many players the feel of their guitar is simply dictated by the height of the strings from the frets and fingerboard but that's only one third of the story.

And it's not all down to how your bridge is adjusted either, without good neck relief the best bridge in the world isn't going to make you love that guitar. Most importantly a low string height doesn't suit a Telecaster but a high action certainly doesn't suit a Jackson King V.

Is your action set correctly?

Now this depends a little on how your guitar has been set up. As a rule of thumb, hold the low E string at the second fret and tap the string midway between the nut and the first fret. You should hear a satisfying click as the string taps the first fret. If you don't then the nut is cut too low. If you have to tap too hard then the nut is set too high.

To check neck relief. Stop the low E string at the first and the twelfth frets and try to slip a plain 0.08 gauge string between the fifth fret and the low E string. If you can't then the neck has a convex bow and requires less tension. Too much of a gap (0.10 or more) means that the guitar has a concave bow. Measure string height with a steel rule with 0.5 mm graduations. String height at the 12th fret (low E) should be between 2.0 and 3.0 mm. String height at the 12th fret for the top E string should be 1.5 – 2.5 mm depending on the nature of your guitar and how you like to play. If you have diffi-

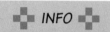 **INFO**

Neck relief is the distance between the fingerboard at its lowest point (7th fret) and the bottom of a string

Neck pitch is the angle of the neck as it leaves the body at the heel

Checking action at the nut

culty seeing the divisions on a small scale steel rule use a car spark gap feeler gauge to estimate the gap.

If you think your action is set too high, check neck relief and nut height before adjusting the height of the bridge or bridge saddles. Remember that no amount of height adjustment at the bridge can compensate for either poor neck relief (truss rod adjustment) or neck pitch. If your bridge is as low as it can go but the action along the neck seems too high then the neck angle needs adjusting.

Some Fender guitars from around the 1970's have a small grub screw through the neck plate which can be used to tilt the neck without removing the strings. Other guitars with a neck plate require the neck to be removed completely and thin shims added or removed to adjust the pitch. Glued or jointed necks need professional attention.

The most important thing to remember is that if you find yourself making an adjustment of more than 2 mm either way, the problem is more likely to be elsewhere in the guitar. Like a car or a bike, the way your guitar plays is the result of many different factors working together – not just one simple adjustment!

Scale

Nope, scales aren't just something you put in the bathroom. The scale of your guitar is an important specification, indeed it has more than a little bearing on the tone and character of the guitar sound. Scale refers to the scale length – the distance in inches from the guitar bridge to the guitar nut. Most contemporary guitars are built with a scale length of between 24 and 26 inches.

Fender Stratocaster and Telecaster guitars have a long scale of 25 1/2 inches. Paul Reed Smith opts for the middle ground of exactly 25 inches while Gibson Les Paul guitars have a scale of 24 3/4 inches. Acoustic guitars also have a long scale, usually around 25 1/2 or 26 inches.

Table of guitar scale

Model	Scale length (inches)
Carvin AC175	25
Epiphone Les Paul Standard	25 (635mm)
Fender 69 Mustang	24
Fender Bajo Sexto Telecaster	30.2 (baritone)
Fender Duo-Sonic	22.7
Fender D Aquisto Ultra	25.125 (638mm)
Fender Reissue Telecaster	25.5 (648mm)
Fender Robben Ford Elite	24.625 (625.5mm)
Fender Standard Stratocaster	25.5
Gretsch Duo Jet	24.5
Gretsch White Falcon	25.5
Pensa Jazz guitar	24 3/4
Schecter Tempest	25.5
Taylor 410	25.5
Taylor Acoustic Bass	34
Tanglewood Baretta	25.5
Tanglewood Ranger Bass	34
Traveler Ace	24.75
Valley Arts Blues	24 3/4

Radius

The curvature of your fingerboard in section is defined as the radius. Fender Telecaster and Stratocaster guitars have a radius of 7 1/4 inches while Gibson guitars have a radius of 12 inches. A larger radius means a wider flatter fingerboard. Some players prefer a flatter fingerboard as it assists techniques such as wide rock style vibrato and allows the string height to be set very close to the fingerboard.

Fender guitar necks have more curvature, thinner fingerboards and closer strings, easier for double stopping and country techniques but harder for long expressive passages.

Acoustic guitars have a large radius, classical guitars have flat fingerboards with no radius at all. To make things even more complicated some guitars with Floyd Rose or Khaler tremolo bridges have a compound radius, a neck with a combination of radius to facilitate faster fingering. Instruments to measure radius are available from specialist suppliers, but without one of these, there is no way to accurately measure the radius without physically chopping the neck in half, so you'll usually have to take the manufacturer's word for it.

Top nut

Nope, nothing to do with squirrels. The nut is the small piece of plastic, metal or bone that sits at the top of the neck between the fingerboard and headstock. The nut has six (or twelve or four depending on your guitar) grooves cut into it. These grooves do two things:

- hold the string in the right place for string spacing
- hold the string at the optimum height above the fingerboard for an easy action

The nut is there to stop the open strings, without the nut you would have to keep a barre chord down all the time. Maintenance is not normally required as the nut suffers less wear and tear than the bridge and frets, just wipe some pencil graphite in the slots from time to time if your strings are sticking. If you have a brand new guitar you might find that the nut slots have been cut too thin for the gauge of strings that you use. It is all right to use a small round file to widen the slots but be careful not to cut into the bottom of the nut. The nut raises the open string above the first fret and if you cut too deep you could cause the open string to catch on the frets and buzz.

Floyd Rose style locking top nut

Some guitars, such as the Vigier and some old Mosrite electric guitars, have a 'zero fret' which simply leaves the job of string spacing to the nut while taking over the task of keeping the open string at the right height above the fingerboard. It can affect the guitar's tone, making open strings sound a little brighter, but in general it's not popular amongst builders.

Guitar nuts can be made of any suitable hard material. The material is important as the nut, like the bridge, is one of the only two points stopping an open (vibrating) string. Therefore, the material that the nut is made of must be acoustically pleasing. In general this means a hard dense material with excellent low friction and which can be easily worked. Only a few man made materials and a few natural materials have these qualities. Bone is considered the best.

If your guitar has a high performance tremolo system you'll know how frustrating it is when the guitar goes out of tune after a heavy session of dive-bombing. To fix this some guitars with tremolo systems feature special systems to enable the string to glide through the nut without resistance while remaining in place.

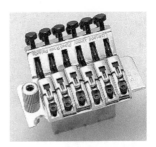

Other high performance tremolo systems, such as the Floyd Rose, have a locking nut. This type of nut traps the string just behind the nut to ensure that the string cannot slip away from the tuning machine while the tremolo arm is depressed. The drawback of this type of system is that if you break a string you have to reach for your toolkit to release the Allen key that is holding the string clamp! Some ESP models feature 'Fliplatch Nuts' which attempt to hold the string in place under a thumb cam.

Floyd Rose style bridge with locking nuts – pic courtesy FCN

Materials commonly used in the manufacture of guitar top nuts

Man made	Natural
Brass	
Steel	Bone
Micarta	Graphite
Corion	Mother-of-pearl
TUSQ	

(courtesy of The Guitar Builders FAQ)

Bone
Currently the material of choice in high quality instruments. It is very hard and offers superior tone, polishes well, and allows precise slot filing.

Corion
A new material with comparable hardness and appearance of bone. Corion offers excellent tone and polishes well. This is the same material found in kitchen and bathroom counter tops.

Micarta
Micarta is a synthetic ivory/bone substitute. Ivory in colour and softer than bone, it files and sands very easily.

Graphite
A self-lubricating material excellent for non-locking tremolo systems.

Mother-of-pearl
Very dense and known for tonal brilliance and beauty.

TUSQ
TUSQ is a man made ivory substitute aimed at acoustic and vintage guitars. TUSQ has improved sustain and clarity.

Neck, fingerboard and frets

Guitar necks come in three types:

bolt on
jointed
straight through

Strats, Super Strats and Teles have bolt on necks, as do some budget Les Paul Studio style models. Les Paul Standard models always have jointed necks with the neck dovetailing into the guitar body at the heel. Gibson 335, some PRS and contemporary instruments such as the Brian Moore MC1 and guitars by JJ Hucke use a 'straight through' approach with hollow 'wings' next to a central core of wood into which the neck, pickups, bridge and headstock are all set. Manufacturers use this method when they want to create a guitar with maximum 'sustain' (the length of time that a note will sound). As the neck and bridge are anchored to the same piece of wood the sustain is said to be longer.

Guitar necks are usually made of maple or mahogany. Each wood is chosen for its tonal qualities. Maple has a brighter sound while mahogany seems to produce a darker tone. In front of the neck is the fingerboard which is often made of a contrasting wood, maple fingerboard on ash neck, rosewood fingerboard on mahogany or ash, ebony on mahogany. You very rarely see a guitar with a maple fingerboard on a mahogany neck.

Glue versus bolt on

There's some snobbery among guitar manufacturers about makers who use bolt on neck systems rather than a traditional wooden joint. There are pro's and cons for each method:

Bolt on pros
* Easier (means cheaper) manufacture.
* Easier repair and adjustment.
* Choose a different fingerboard without choosing a new guitar!.

Bolt on cons
* Bulky heel as bolts need good base.
* Some chance of neck movement.
* Possibility of problems under pressure and temperature changes.

Jointed pros
* Smoother heel.
* Possibility of more vibration transmitted from neck to body.
* Looks much better.

Jointed cons
* If the neck breaks, it's an expensive repair!
* No method of adjustment.

This Peavey Cirrus bass has a straight through neck

Frets

To play a note in tune you need to shorten the length of the string by 'stopping' the string on the fingerboard. The exact place you need to stop the string is pretty precise and very complicated (see table below). You could stop the string yourself (no fret) like a violin player but that's pretty hard with a barre chord, and violin strings are much thicker, so the gui-

Bead

Tang

Cross section of a fret

tarist uses frets to allow precise intonation anywhere on the fingerboard.

Guitar frets are small pieces of nickel silver or steel alloy wire set into the neck at points dictated by a precise mathematical formula. The fret is made of one piece of metal in a T shape. The bead (or crown) is the part which you see on top of the fingerboard. The tang sits in a slot in the fingerboard and anchors the fret to the guitar.

Guitars are tuned using something called the 'equal tempered scale'. This gives us 12 semitones in an octave. This scale also determines the distance between frets. There's a special mathematical 'rule of 18' (in reality 17.817) which allows us to calculate fret spacing. The distance to the first fret from the nut is calculated by dividing the total scale length by 17.817.

For a 25 1/2 in. scale...

25.5 / 17.817 = 1.431273 (or 1.431)

That result is then subtracted from the total scale length

25.5 − 1.431 = 24.069

That result is divided by 17.817 to get the distance from the first fret to the second...

24.069 / 17.817 = 1.351

.. and so on

(Courtesy of the guitar builders FAQ)

Position markers

Every guitar has a point along the neck exactly half way between bridge and nut. This is the twelfth fret, in musical terms the 'octave'. The twelfth fret always has a special position marker, sometimes a particularly ornate piece of inlay, maybe even the musician's or manufacturer's name. Most commonly the twelfth fret simply has two dots instead of one.

Other key points are the fifth and seventh fret. To make this easier to remember, many guitars have fret markers. A fret marker is a little pointer which shows you where the most important positions are. Many people (me included) get so used to having these markers around that if we play a guitar without markers, we get lost and confused. Most guitars with fret markers also have dots on the side of the fingerboard at the same position as the fret markers on the fingerboard.

✚ *INFO* ✚

Spanish musicians sometimes needed to remember where to put their fingers so tied rags around the necks of their instruments at specific points. This is how the fret marker came about.

Strings

Stand by for Richard Riley's money saving tip of the year!! Don't buy a new amp or even a new effects pedal until you've bought some new strings! Because your strings start to deteriorate from the moment you put them on. The worst news is that if you play live you should be thinking about swapping strings at the end of every other gig. That's because your fingers produce enough sweat and acid to eat through your strings in no time. Dead strings have dead spots, poor magnetism (no volume), woolly tone and no chance of any flash. Change 'em .. NOW!

Strings are supplied by the gauge of the top (high E) string in thousands of an inch. Players often choose a gauge depending on the sort of music they like to play; metal – 0.008, country – 0.10 etc. In truth the gauge you need depends on your guitar and the way you have it set. Nevertheless, here's another rule for your thumb:

Typical string gauges

Rock and shred high gain soloists	.008 .010 .015 .021 .028 .039 (X light)
Rock and thrash lead players	.009 .011 .016 .024 .032 .042 (light – more volume)
Rock and grunge	.010 .013 .017 .026 .036 .046 (med-light better for power chords)
Metal and blues	.010 .013 .017 .030 .042 .052 (heavy bottom for good low end response)

Guitar and bass strings are made from two pieces of wire; a steel core and nickel or alloy windings. A machine is used to spin the core at high tension as the windings are carefully wrapped along the length of the string. Electric guitar strings are commonly made from NPS (nickel plated steel) although nickel strings are becoming popular again. In the 1950's guitar strings were usually made from plain nickel, nowadays the demand for 'retro' or 'aged' sounds is bringing this material back. Guitar strings are also made from Swedish steel or even chrome.

Different materials have different magnetic qualities which affect the sound of the guitar. NPS and stainless steel have a brighter sound than plain nickel. Chrome is often used in the manufacture of flatwound strings which are popular with jazz players. A chrome flatwound string has a darker sound than a roundwound string. Swedish rock band The Cardigans prefer flatwound strings for recording. Plain strings (usually G,

Profiles of several string types

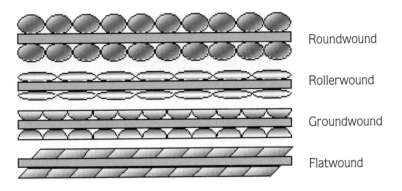

Roundwound

Rollerwound

Groundwound

Flatwound

B, E) are usually made of stainless steel as this resists corrosion. Some string sets even include an additional high E string for luck.

* While the central core has a common profile, the windings can be altered to affect the way the guitar plays and sounds.
* The most common type of guitar string is 'roundwound'. Roundwound strings are very bright and are commonly used for rock guitar.
* Rollerwound strings are midway between roundwound and groundwound. They are popular with jazz and fusion players as they offer less finger resistance and a mellow tone.
* Halfwound (or 'groundwound') strings feature windings which have been ground flat after the string has been wound. This produces a softer tone.
* Flatwound strings are wound with a flat ribbon of wire. These strings are very smooth to the touch and have almost no winding noise at all. The flatwound string produces a very dark sound which is popular with traditional jazz players.

An American company 'Elixir' has just started to market 'Polyweb' strings. These are traditional roundwound strings with plastic filler between each winding. The aim is to lengthen the life and sound of the string by resisting corrosion introduced into the windings by the guitarist's fingertips.

Roundwound	NPS	rock guitar
Half round (ground)	NPS	rock bass
Flatwound	Chrome	jazz guitar

The magnetic qualities of nickel and steel dictate their usefulness for electric guitars with magnetic pickups. Acoustic guitar players with piezo or contact pickups use non magnetic brass, bronze or phosphor bronze alloy strings. Brass has a very bright sound while bronze and phosphor bronze alloy strings are most popular, having a combination of a bright tone with good volume. Bronze and phosphor bronze strings also last longer than pure brass.

Strings and intonation

Your guitar must have a good set of strings or you will not be able to play in tune, especially as you move up the fingerboard. Players of non-fretted instruments are able to compensate for irregularities in string diameter and bridge placing by moving their fingers a fraction up or down the neck until they can find the correct place to play in tune. This is called 'Intonation' or the art of remaining in tune anywhere on the fingerboard of the instrument. Guitarists on the other hand are trapped by the immovable fret which cannot be adjusted to compensate for varying string sizes or high action. Therefore the guitar must have a mechanical device to compensate for this on the player's behalf.

For instance, as the diameter of a string increases, the length of the string needed to play in tune decreases by a fraction taking the guitar fractionally out of tune. A solution was required if the guitar was to be a successful recording instrument. One of the very first adjustable electric guitar bridges was developed by Leo Fender at the time that he was designing the innovative Telecaster (nee Broadcaster) electric guitar. His bridge is still efficient at compensating for the varying thickness of guitar strings by employing movable bridge pieces which can be moved up, down, backwards or forwards by tiny amounts to compensate for the differing diameters of plain and wound strings. In this way the guitar player is able to play anywhere on the fingerboard and remain in tune.

Machine heads

Before guitars had metal parts they were tuned like a violin with friction pegs through the headstock. Geared tuners started to appear in the early part of this century in response to the guitarists demand for stable tunings, especially with the guitar soloist just around the corner. The response to this demand was the tuning machine or tuning head. This is a geared device with a high geared cog turning a screw attached to the tuning peg. The tuning head is usually geared 12:1 or 14:1, i.e.12 or 14 turns of the button will cause the peg to move through one revolution. The high gear means that a good degree of accuracy can be used when tuning the guitar, although the accuracy can be impaired by a worn gear or screw. Any movement in this area can enable the peg to slip and make tuning difficult.

Sealed tuning machines are most desirable as they come filled with grease or oil which acts as a damping and moisture repelling agent. Of the sealed tuners choose die cast enclosed heads above the cheaper pressed covers. Tuning machines with a pressed cover can be identified as the cover isn't fitted tightly around the peg. This design enables dirt and moisture to penetrate inside the mechanism so machines of this sort must be replaced more often than sealed tuning machines. Classical and folk guitars often have tuning machines with exposed gears.

Tuning machines are easily maintained. Periodically some small adjustment might be needed to tighten the tension screw at the top of the button – worth checking every month or so as the head will need to be replaced if the screw is lost.

Tuning machines with a pressed metal cover need a spot of 3:1 oil from time to time but sealed die cast units don't require any maintenance other than an occasional tightening of the tension screw on each button. This simply adds resistance to the mechanism but will not stop a worn gear from slipping. The screw should be slightly more than finger tight. If a die cast head fails to turn, check the tension screw for over-tightening. The popularity of large tremolo dive bombs and swirls, coupled with

INFO

Early tailpieces were often called 'Compensator' tailpieces because of this need to compensate for string thickness.

Movable bridge pieces allow accurate tuning

Sealed tuning machine

Pressed steel tuning machine

Locking machine heads from Gotoh lock the string automatically without any extra string winds – pic courtesy FCN

many guitar players' obsession with tying the string immovably to the guitar has prompted manufacturers do develop tuning machines which trap the guitar string to the peg. Manufacturers such as Sperzel and Gotoh have machine heads which tighten as the string tension increases. The aim is always to prevent the string from slipping and going out of tune as the result of heavy tremolo use.

Re-stringing your guitar

Stringing up
Remove one string at a time to maintain tension on the neck, some players even remove strings in the order 6,1,5,2,4,3 to counter the loss of tension. Use a small pair of cutters to remove the curly peg end and ball end if necessary from the old string in order to take it from the guitar. Take care when removing the string and don't whisk an old string through a tremolo or stop bar bridge, the spinning end of the string can seriously mar the finish.

Tying on
The aim is to have just the right amount of turns on the peg head. Too many and the string will wind over itself, too few and slipping is inevitable. Here's a table of turns for a regular electric guitar with 0.10 strings.

Table of string turns for an electric guitar

String	Turns
E	2.5 turns
A	3.5
D	5.5
G (plain)	5.5
B	7.5
E	7.5

Actually getting this number of turns takes a little experience, the art is knowing just how much spare string to leave on the other side of the peg head before you make the first turn. This is tricky as different manufacturers use different string lengths, and these even vary from set to set. As a rule of thumb leave 8 – 10cm of slack at the bridge when you bend the string into the peg head for your first turn. When fitting the new string make sure that the ball end is firmly seated in the underside of the bridge before measuring up at the peg end. Give the new string a couple of quick pulls and use the tremolo arm (if necessary) to move the bridge and make sure that the ball end isn't snagged elsewhere.

Pet peeve time

OK. I keep reading these magazines where some guy says; 'To absolutely prevent slipping, take the string through the peg head, turn in back on itself, tie a double sheep shank with a quarter whirl then bake in a warm oven for 40 minutes ...' Norks mate. Strings slip because there is nothing sticking them to the peg head – that magical ingredient is friction. The only way to increase friction is to increase surface area and that means getting more string wrapped around the peg head.

The key is getting enough windings on to the peg head without the windings over lapping, (see the table above). When the string is correctly on the peg head stretch the string away from the body like a bow and pull gently. Then tune and repeat, tune and repeat until there's no more slip-page left. Strings low E to G are guaranteed not to break if you do this, B and high E need to be treated with a little more care – if they do break change your brand! In twenty years of playing I have only broken two while stretching like this and they were both from an old set.

A simple stretch job like this will cure no end of apparent hardware problems – from slipping tuning heads to a poorly adjusted tremolo. In fact if everybody did this one little thing we'd all save hundreds of pounds in buying new machine heads that we just didn't need! Yes, this one simple act will set you apart from the masses by turning you into a super hero in the eyes of your guitar technician who will no longer be to blame when your guitar is out of tune.

Pet hate time

You've met my pet peeve, well here's my pet hate (I'm a well balanced person – chip on each shoulder!) Please, please cut the strings from your headstock. I'm a mess of scratches from guitarists who leave curly wire hanging from the ends of their guitar. I promise that you strings will not slip through the peg head if you do (if you string your guitar properly anyway). So give your guitar a hair cut!

The best thing to do for your string winding technique is to invest in a string winder. This simple device sits over the tuning peg and enables you to rapidly wind the string around the peg head. Because there's very little

Strings tied neatly onto the tuning machines

effort involved in winding this way more attention can be given to the tension of the string as it is wound on, adding to the effectiveness of your restringing job. Save your wrist and cut stringing time in half with one of these little beauties. You haven't got one already? Go and buy one ... now!

A string winder saves effort

4 ❖

Pickups and electronics

Pickup history

Landmark events in pickup history begin in the early part of this century with innovators and inventors who experimented with phonograph horns and microphones mounted on acoustic guitars. Possibly the most notable of these is Lloyd Loar, an employee of Gibson from 1919 to 1924 he is (almost) famous for experimenting with innovative dual bridge 'Vivi-Tone' guitars which could either be played electrically or acoustically via a system of levers.

Invention of the single coil pickup is credited to Paul Barth and George Beauchamp of Los Angeles California simply because they patented their design first (No; 2,089,171 filed 1934, granted August 10 1937), although many people are known to have been experimenting with pickups around this time. Beauchamp's patent application took three years to be granted because the patent office didn't know whether their guitar was a musical instrument or an electrical device.

However, a pickup isn't much good without an instrument, so George Beauchamp co-founded the Electro String Company with Adolph Rickenbacher. Together they made Rickenbacher guitars (changed to Rickenbacker to avoid confusion) and the Barth and Beauchamp pickup was incorporated into the Electro String Co.'s innovative aluminium bodied A-22 model 'Frying Pan' guitar.

The A-22 guitar with pickup sold for $62.50 and proved commercially successful throughout the 1930s and 40s when another young inventor picked up the baton. Leo Fender knew of Rickenbacher's work through his partner 'Doc' Kauffman, an ex Electro String employee, and through Rickenbacker amps. Leo Fender's first single coil pickup was patented in 1944 and remains the standard in single coil design to this day.

On the other side of the coin, the humbucking pickup was invented by Seth Lover, although other less successful designs had existed before then. Seth Lover was another young electronics enthusiast who left a career in auto-electrics to join Gibson in 1941. He invented the 'PAF' humbucking pickup in 1955 along with numerous other amps and effects before moving to Fender in 1967. Seth Lover died in 1997. Adolph Richenbacher died March 1976

Magnetic pickups

Conventional magnetic guitar pickups convert motion from the vibrating string into energy in the form of alternating electric current. This current is ultimately turned by loudspeaker into air vibrations which we hear as music. Of course if we were standing right next to the guitar we wouldn't need to do all this. But we wouldn't have gigs, records or video either. So to broadcast the guitar sound we need to 'pick up' the sound of the guitar and turn it into a form that can be transmitted electronically. This is the function of the guitar pickup and the microphone.

The magnetic pickup senses the string vibration through electro-magnetic induction and not by sensing or reproducing the sound wave that is naturally created at the same time when the string is plucked or hit. It would even be possible to play the guitar in space (with a special spacesuit!) as the electro-magnetic pickup would work just as well, even though sound waves cannot travel in a vacuum. The guitar may even sound better than it would on earth as the motion of the string would not be impeded by the moving air.

How a magnetic pickup works

INFO

The hertz (Hz) is the unit of frequency. It is named after the scientist H.R Hertz 1857-1894)

It's important at this stage to know a little about string vibration. A guitar string vibrates in a figure of eight movement. Each complete figure of eight is one 'cycle'. If the string has been pulled tight the figure of eight becomes smaller. A guitar string that completes one figure of eight 440 times every second (one 'cycle' per second or Hz) produces 440 sound waves which our ear hears as the note of A. So A is 440Hz or one figure of eight 440 times every second.

An electric guitar is designed so that each metal string passes through a strong magnetic field produced by a magnet contained within a pickup device lying below the strings. Vibrations produced by the string disturb magnetic 'lines of force' created naturally by the magnet. These disturbances in turn induce a small electric current in a coil of thin copper wire surrounding the magnet. As the string moves closer to the magnet the current in the coil flows in one direction. As the string moves away from the magnet and returns to the top of the figure of eight the current flows in the opposite direction. This is how alternating current is generated inside the pickup.

The frequency and direction of the current flow is dictated by the frequency of the vibration of the string. In this way, pitch information, in the form of electrical impulses, is transmitted to the amplifier. Tone and amplitude (volume) information is transmitted as voltage created by the strength of the electrical impulses which get fainter as the string gradually returns to a resting position. Thus the magnetic pickup detects changes in a magnetic field which it translates to a current that can be amplified. Pole pieces concentrate the magnetic field and help the player (or technician) installing the pickup to place the magnet in just the right point under the string.

All these signals are carried to the amplifier and finally appear as sound

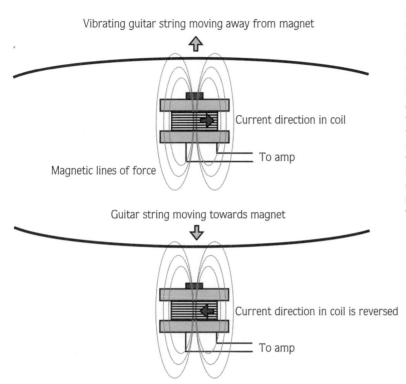

Vibrating guitar string moving away from magnet

Current direction in coil

To amp

Magnetic lines of force

Guitar string moving towards magnet

Current direction in coil is reversed

To amp

How a magnetic pickup works: vibrations produced by the string disturb magnetic 'lines of force' created naturally by the magnet. These disturbances in turn induce a small electric current in a coil of thin copper wire surrounding the magnet. As the string moves closer to the magnet the current in the coil flows in one direction. As the string moves away from the magnet the current flows in the opposite direction

vibrations in a reverse of the same process by which they were picked up. An electrical coil surrounds a magnet which is attached to a speaker cone. Alternating current in the coil pushes the magnet first one way and then back when the current flows in the opposite direction. This in turn causes the speaker cone to produce sound waves and reproduce the information that the magnetic pickup sensed from the vibrating string.

Project

Take an ordinary PP3 battery and connect it to the terminals of a loudspeaker. The cone of the loudspeaker will move out or in depending on the 'polarity' of the connections. If you now reverse the polarity the speaker will move in the other direction. If you were able to do this 440 times a second you'd produce a note, the note of A. The note is produced as the speaker cone causes the air to vibrate at 440 times a second.

Alnico and ceramic magnets

Magnets are measured according to strength in 'gauss', after the German mathematician KF Gauss (1777 – 1855). Most modern magnetic pickups use magnets made from a combination of three different metals; Aluminium, Nickel and Cobalt. These together form 'Alnico' a powerful magnetic material. Alnico magnets are rated numerically by strength according to specifications. Alnico 5 (12.5k Gauss) and Alnico 8 (8k Gauss) magnets are often used in guitar pickups. Gibson has used Alnico 2,4,5 and 8 in pickups. Fender pickups often use Alnico 5 magnets of around 4k Gauss.

Ceramic magnets (Arnox and Indox) are made from clay which has been combined with metallic particles and made magnetic. Ceramic magnets have a higher output and brighter sound and are cheaper to produce than conventional Alnico magnets, although the continuing desire for an 'authentic vintage' sound means that Alnico loaded pickups still remain popular. Budget Chinese pickups are often fitted with bar magnets for economy.

Pickup construction

The strength and sound (frequency response) of a pickup is not dictated simply by magnet strength, coil resistance or the number and shape of the coils. A coil with many windings around a weaker magnet will produce a pickup with good bass response and a warm 'blue' sound. A stronger magnet with a coil with less windings and so less resistance will produce a pickup with a good treble sound. It's no surprise that humbucking pickups which have many windings help to give the Les Paul its trademark blues sound while the Fender single coil pickup is associated with country and clear picking.

The physical dimensions of the pole pieces also play an important point in determining how the pickup will respond. Magnetic pole pieces concentrate the magnetic field under the strings – a broad pole piece will help

A single coil pickup

Interior of Yamaha double coil pickup showing wooden spacers

the pickup produce a high output sound, and smaller pole pieces produce a smoother less aggressive sound. Adjustable pole pieces are important if you often change the height of your strings or want to fine tune the response of your pickups to your playing style. If the pole piece is closer to the strings the pickup will produce more output although the note often loses definition.

Many different factors must be taken into account when evaluating or describing how a pickup will sound. For instance every magnetic pickup relies on the vibrations of the metal string. A dirty or badly made string will have an enormous effect on the sound of the guitar. Additionally pickups gradually lose their magnetism over time, and no two pickups will fade in exactly the same way. It's this character that determines the sound of old pickups and dictates that no two will ever sound the same. For many players this 'aged' sound is very desirable.

Single coil pickup

The design of the single coil pickup uses one coil of wire around six pole pieces and just two conductors. The pole pieces are often staggered in height or adjustable to enable the volume of individual strings to be balanced for an even output. The entire pickup can be raised or lowered using the height adjusting screws on each side. This pickup has a very clear sound with a lower electrical output than a dual coil model. Some disadvantages are that the design is very receptive to mains hum, interference from radio waves, computer monitors and even fluorescent lights as it does not incorporate any kind of noise rejection.

INFO

*P*ickup manufacturers such as Seymour Duncan now produce artificially 'aged' pickups which attempt to recreate the sound of a pickup made forty or fifty years ago.

INFO

*S*ome pickups made to fit into a regular single coil pickup slot have humbucking qualities. Examples of these are the DiMarzio 'The Cruiser' and 'Virtual Vintage'

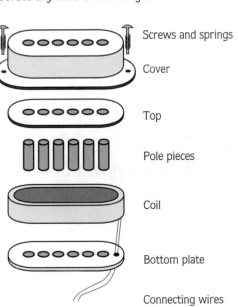

Screws and springs

Cover

Top

Pole pieces

Coil

Bottom plate

Connecting wires

Exploded view of a single coil pickup

Double coil 'humbucking' pickups

Double coil pickups have two magnets and two coils of wire – essentially two single coil pickups in one case. The name 'double' or 'dual' coil has now been largely over taken by simple description of 'humbucker' which although it is a Gibson invention is used in the same way as 'Hoover' – a generic term passing into common vocabulary. Humbucking pickups are easily identifiable by their large size and often the exposed bobbins make the double coil construction obvious.

Exploded view of double coil humbucking pickup

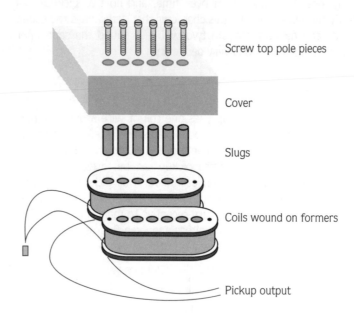

Screw top pole pieces

Cover

Slugs

Coils wound on formers

Pickup output

Humbucking pickup by JHS

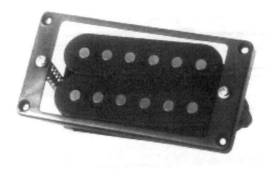

Development of the humbucker

Like any forward looking manufacturer, the Gibson guitar company needed to innovate to stay ahead and were first to recognise the problems with single coil pickups. After experimenting with a humbucking amplifier Gibson employee Seth Lover invented the humbucking pickup in which two coils are placed side by side but connected 'out of phase' meaning that the inner side of one coil connects to the outer side of the other. This has the effect of cancelling out the signal – and cancelling out any hum too. However because of the way that the magnets are aligned, string motion picked up by the magnetic poles is amplified, not cancelled. The effect is to cancel any residual hum from the coils while accentuating the signal picked up by the magnetic pole pieces. In this way the humbucking pickup may completely cancel out any mains (electrical) hum picked up by the coils. However the humbucking pickup can be affected by hum at twice the mains frequency, so the pickup must be shielded with a metal cover to reduce the risk of any interference.

The humbucker design was patented by Seth Lover and Gibson in 1959 but his pickups were fitted to Gibson guitars from 1955. In the interim period between, the humbucking pickup was given a sticker to

Hiw a humbuckwer works

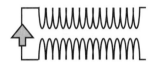

Movement of string
induces current in coil

Hum induced is cancelled
because coils are wound
out of phase. Signal
is unaffected.

DiMarzio PAF® classic
pickup (Courtesy Larry
DiMarzio/ DiMarzio Inc)

identify the pickup as a Gibson invention and to warn copyists that the patent was pending (in the hands of the infamous US Government Patent Office in other words).

These famous pickups are now known as PAF® pickups and can be identified by a small sticker ('Patent Applied For' or 'Patent Number 2,737,842') applied to the base of the pickup. Pickups from this period are highly prized by collectors for their sound and authenticity, and a guitar which features a pair of these pickups will be very valuable. However, as they are now nearly fifty years old, the chances of any undiscovered PAF pickups arriving on the open market are extremely slim.

Today, the only sure method of determining a real PAF from a fake would be to disassemble the pickup, examine the components and match the electrical characteristics with those of a certified genuine Gibson PAF pickup from the correct period. No collector is going to allow casual surgery of such a prized antique however, so fakes abound. Incidentally, many pickup manufacturers make their own PAF pickups, underlining the fact that one cream and one black bobbin is no indication of original Gibson authenticity.

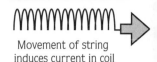

INFO

Some people claim that a PAF pickup can be recognised by its distinctive two colour (cream and black) coil bobbins. However production shortages meant this colour scheme changed frequently from all black to cream and black to cream and back again.

Hybrid pickups

Seymour Duncan and DiMarzio both produce humbucking pickups in a single coil shape. This enables the player to change a single coil pickup for a humbucker without the need for potentially devaluing work on the guitar.

Other pickups, including the Seymour Duncan Hot Rails® and the DiMarzio Fast Track®, are single coil style humbuckers with four conductors for Coil Split, Coil Tap and Out Of Phase sounds, much more than is available from a conventional single coil pickup.

Players who use light strings are often at a disadvantage with pickups that were designed fifty years ago for very heavy strings. DiMarzio's X2N pickup has two very large blade pole pieces which magnetise the string at any point above the pickup with few dead spots. The X2N is one of the highest output pickups available, although DiMarzio's experience in pickup building enables the X2N to produce a clear and bright sound even from light strings.

EMG pickups

EMG Inc. is rightly famous for its range of innovative pickups which incorporate a small pre-amp into the pickup case, no external circuitry other than a conventional battery is required. The result is a low noise, high output pickup with much greater signal strength than a conventional magnetic pickup. This benefits the player by allowing the use of longer cables with little line loss. Some amps – particularly tube amps – also benefit from a little overdrive at the input stage.

'Lace' Pickups

'Lace Sensor' is a trademark of Actodyne General Incorporated. The Lace Sensor pickup is a conventional magnetic pickup with a peculiar 'inside out' arrangement of coil and magnets. Unlike a conventional pickup in which the coil surrounds the magnet, in a Lace pickup two ceramic magnets lie each side of a metal bobbin shaped like two 'U back to back around which the coil is wound. A further three magnets lie underneath the coil. The bobbin replaces the pole pieces allowing the pickup to have a much wider magnetic 'window' underneath the strings.

The pickup is much quieter than the traditional single coil and pole piece design with a warmer sound from a slightly thicker coil (7.1 kilohms resistance, the traditional Stratocaster pickup has a resistance of around 6 kilohms). Additional benefits include a small shock mount on the base of the pickup to reduce acoustic feedback and low energy magnets which don't have as much string damping properties.

Piezoelectric transducer bridges

A fairly recent development is the fitting of two pickup systems to an electric guitar. For many years the crystal 'piezo' pickup has been used in acoustic/electric guitars, but in 1994 Parker produced the first guitar to have both conventional magnetic pickups and a set of piezo equipped bridge pieces. Guitars with this system can be amplified using either system or a combination of both. The piezo equipped bridge picks up vibrations directly from the strings, unlike the magnetic pickup which requires the string to disturb a magnetic field. In this way the player can use both distinctive sounds on the guitar.

Mike Christian produces a range of piezoelectric bridge saddles for Les Paul and Stratocaster guitars enabling the player to blend the acoustic and electric sounds of their instrument. This kind of system needs major structural modifications to the guitar including additional routing for on board pre-amps etc., but the range of sounds available is unequalled by any other system.

Acoustic guitar pickups

Acoustic guitarists need to connect to amps and mixing desks but often want to hold onto the original appearance of their instrument. To this end acoustic guitars can either have a contact pickup or 'bug' invisibly attached to the guitar, or a temporary magnetic pickup can be attached to the sound hole just underneath the strings. A small contact pickup (Barcus Berry or DiMarzio) is sometimes attached to the soundboard of the guitar, but this isn't as common as it used to be as electronic devices get smaller and public demand for high quality amplified sound becomes greater.

Many acoustic players use guitars with factory fitted piezoelectric pickup and preamp systems. Almost every acoustic guitar manufacturer includes at least one model with this kind of system in their catalogue. Examples include Takamine ESG-45c, Yamaha APX10A, Ovation Standard Balladeer, etc.

The Fishman onboard pre-amp has volume and tone controls

The advantages to the player of a factory fitted system are that the manufacturer is able to design the pickup system to suit the model and that installation is done while the guitar is being manufactured.

Contact pickups, 'strapjacks' and 'hot-dots'

For high end acoustic guitars, such as those made by Taylor and Martin (which might cost £3,000 – £5,000), another system has to be employed. The owner of one of these guitars will insist that the pickup system is installed with no adverse effects to the finish or acoustic sound of the guitar. This is a real problem for pickup manufacturers, and several approaches have been attempted.

Contact pickups are small encapsulated piezo electric transducers which are either permanently hidden inside the instrument or temporarily fixed with glue or putty to the bridge (this area is usually not lacquered). Popular examples are Barcus Berry or the DiMarzio 'Acoustic Model' If the pickup is permanently installed inside the guitar, very often a 'Strapjack'

Battery pack for acoustic on board pre-amp – pics courtesy FCN end pin will be used. This device replaces the strap button at the base of the acoustic guitar with a combination jack socket and strap button. The jack socket installs right through the end block inside the guitar which has the advantage of being both discreet and very strong. All the wiring is hidden away inside the guitar the only clue to the presence of the 'hot dot' being the enlarged strap button.

Mimesis

Contact pickups often don't produce the sound quality that many people require because of the way that the pickup is attached to the guitar. Many people dislike using the adhesives that are needed to attach the contact pickup, and the contact pickup can't reproduce the sound of the moving air produced by the acoustic guitar, the very sound that gives the guitar its character. The Mimesis Blend pickup by Mike Vanden is a semi-conventional magnetic pickup system which clamps harmlessly to the inside of the guitar sound hole. The pickup is powered by a small 3.5V camera battery which attaches to the underside of the pickup – no external preamp is necessary. The same company produces another similar pickup which has a small microphone on a gooseneck. The microphone picks up the acoustic sound of the guitar and the player is able to blend this with sound from the magnetic pickup by means of a small rotary pot.

Vintage pickups

The sound of any pickup is a combination of several variables. These include the tension of the wire as it was wound into a coil, the varying strengths of identical magnets and even the proximity of a magnetic pickup to another magnetic field such as a guitar amp power transformer when the guitar is stored.

Modern pickup manufacturers are now able to smooth out the production of pickups to ensure that quality remains at a uniform standard, but this wasn't always the case. For the first few years of Fender pickup production pickups were wound by hand by many operators – some more skilled than others. This means old Fender pickups vary wildly in terms of DC resistance, frequency response and output. Pickups were even wound back to front, upside down or wound the right way up with the magnets put in upside down!. All this added to the character of those old Fender guitars but made choosing a good one a tricky operation. This individual nature is part of the reason that buying an old Fender must involve many trips to see as many different guitars as possible.

Recently there has been a trend towards remagnetising old pickups. This involves dismantling the pickup and passing the magnets through a powerful magnetic field to make the pickup louder and more sensitive. However, the character of an old instrument comes from the sound of the pickups which mellow and acquire a unique personality as time passes. It's this sound which defines a vintage guitar and helps it to become valuable. Remagnetising will bring new life to any pickup but at the risk of irreversibly changing the irreplaceable character of the guitar for ever.

Factory pickups and replacements

The pickups that were factory fitted to your guitar were probably chosen by the manufacturer on a value added minus cost basis. In other words how much extra zing the pickups gave your instrument less the cost it took to fit the part. They do this to bring a guitar out at a particular price point. You on the other hand just want the best parts for your guitar, so you don't mind spending a little more on another more expensive pickup. If you want the maker to do this for you it'll cost a heck of a lot more than the stock guitar you just bought, this is why 'custom shop' guitars with your choice of design and fittings cost a load more.

Choosing your replacement pickup

Boy, this is the difficult one. You know what sound you want from your guitar but you know that the sound of your guitar is a combination of things; the pickups, the wood, the amp, the strings, even the way you are feeling today. It's a pretty safe bet that a new pickup will enhance that sound, especially if you are replacing the pickups in an old or budget guitar. The difficulty is; how can you be sure that the pickup you are buying will be the best one for your guitar?

Most of the time pickups are chosen by comparison. In other words a manufacturer might say 'Hey remember the sound of those early 1954 Strat pickups?. Well my Tone-O-Blaster '54's sound just like that!' You don't need to be told that in 1954 Fender were hand winding their pickups and no two ever sounded alike, even on the same guitar. In fact some of the early Strat pickups just sounded terrible!

Another manufacturer might say 'Joe Fastnoodle now uses my pickups – he won't get out of bed for any other!' And, the next time you go see Joe Fastnoodle and his band 'Ten Thousand Notes and Nothing To Say' he'll be using the same guitar that you saw him with five years ago, looking pretty untouched!.

Of course if you go to the store, don't bother asking if pickups are available on a 'try before you buy' basis – nobody wants to sell a second hand pickup. It's a tough one.

So choosing a pickup is luck and judgement. The only thing you have to go on is the advice of the manufacturer. These days some manufacturers such as DiMarzio are publishing specs to help you choose. Specifications can be interpreted in different ways but they are a lot better than nothing when it comes to making your mind up. Every published specification must be looked at alongside the specifications of similar models from another manufacturer. The big three things to watch for are:

* DC resistance
* Output in milliwatts
* Frequency response

DC resistance

This is the resistance of the copper coil surrounding the pickup magnets. The coil carries the current that is induced by the disturbance in the magnetic field caused by string vibrations. A typical single coil pickup will have 8 – 10 thousand turns of wire. A larger coil means (usually) more output. However the increased inductance often means a deeper sound with less highs. So a published DC resistance can be used to give us some idea as to the pickup tone.

Here is a table of pickup models and their DC resistance.

DC resistance and frequency responses of some models of pickup

Model	DC resistance	Frequency response
US DiMarzio PAF®	7.65k	
US Gibson '57 Classic (PAF)®	8.2k	
Seymour Duncan Seth Lover®	8.1k	8.14 kHz
German Schaller S6 Single Coil	6.4k	
Washburn Humbucker (Far East)	8.2k	
1954 Fender Stratocaster®	5.91k	
1958 Fender Stratocaster®	6.41k	
Don Lace 4000 Lace®	5.8k	4.3 kHz
Seymour Duncan Vintage Staggered®	6.5k	10.0 kHz

Notice that the £20 Washburn Humbucker has the same DC resistance as the £120 Gibson replacement. The DC resistance of the Washburn pickup was taken from a review instrument which proved to have a low output although the specs suggest that the coil was the same size (or at least had the same electrical properties) on both pickups. The Gibson pickup has more output and a better tone because the magnet is much stronger than the weak bar magnet in the Chinese pickup, although the coil specs are similar.

To make things even more confusing the tension in the windings can also change DC resistance. For these reasons DC resistance measurements should not be regarded in isolation as a true indicator of how a pickup will sound on your guitar.

Output in milliwatts

DiMarzio publish the output figures of their pickups in milliwatts which enables us to visualise the difference in power between pickups. Their PAF humbucker has a output of 203 milliwatts while the DiMarzio Blue Velvet pickup has an output of just 129 milliwatts.

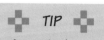
TIP

Your pickup's output must match the input impedance of your amplifier, and although most amps are similar in this respect, the pickup will sound and behave slightly differently depending on your amp's input impedance.

Frequency response

The third factor to take into account when choosing a pickup is that of frequency response. This is now seen as a more accurate way of judging the sound of a pickup, but few manufacturers publish these figures. DiMarzio pickups are rated in the form of amp top controls. So a DiMarzio PAF® has a 'Tone Guide' of 5 (not very trebly), 6 (reasonable midrange) and 7 (good low end). Their Velvet Hammer® pickup has a 'Tone Guide' of 9 (very trebly), 4 (not much middle) and 5 (reasonable bass).

Probably the best source of information is the pickup manufacturer's catalogue. Seymour Duncan has a technical support e-mail address for direct access to specialist technicians and engineers. While you choose your new pickup have a look at what is available and decide what you want based on your guitar and the sound you need then ask the engineers and match as much information as possible to the sound or performance of the pickup you have in mind. It's not an exact science at all.

Pickup combinations

There are no rules to determine which combinations of pickups are allowed on which guitar. As long as you aren't planning on putting your baby into mass production, it's unlikely that anyone will send the lawyers round – just make sure you give them the opportunity to copy it when you get famous!

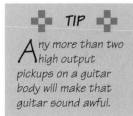

TIP

Any more than two high output pickups on a guitar body will make that guitar sound awful.

The other rule isn't so obvious. You might think that putting loads of pickups on a guitar will make it sound louder, bigger, better, etc. That's not right either. There's just not enough room on a guitar body to give each pickup enough space, so stray magnetic fields just confuse the string by pulling it in all directions at once. If you want the visuals without the hassle then create your very own five pickup Gargantu-mega-gibbo-caster without the expense or the problems of buying and fitting brand new pickups. Make friends with your local guitar shop (you mean you aren't friends already?), hang around on a Saturday afternoon and wait for the naff pickups that their repairman throws out. Take the magnets out and glue the pickup covers onto your guitar then screw the pickup mounting ring on as if it were a real one.

Disclaimer. After years of freelancing for guitar magazines I know this: Somebody somewhere will have a triple necked Les Paul with fifteen stacked humbucking pickups and will swear it sounds amazing. All I can say is if it suits you, then it's priceless.

Guitar electronics

Although the pickups in a guitar would work on their own, the electric guitar is nearly always fitted with some circuitry – at least a volume and tone control – to help the player control the output from the guitar. It's not difficult to understand why, minimalism wasn't popular in the boom days after the second world war and guitar makers weren't alone in stuffing their products with about as many gadgets as they could to take full advantage of the technical revolution. For one maker in particular three pickups, two volume controls and a tone control blew everybody else out of the water in 1954.

Guitar electronics are a great way to get a handle on basic electronic principles. Why? Because there's nothing in most guitars that wasn't invented after 1958 meaning that the mysterious world of the integrated digital circuit and microchip still stands at the door of most guitar designers asking to be invited in. Digital electronics to guitars are sort of like the geeky guys you find in the kitchen at parties. They come in handy when you need to fix the stereo but they aren't really good time guys. You'll find plenty of digital stuff in your guitar effects pedals and amp but the electronics inside the biggest selling guitars in the UK haven't changed in the last 45 years.

Principal electronic components in the electric guitar

Volume control

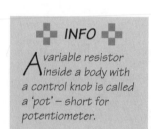

It is useful to be able to turn the guitar down at the guitar instead of legging it across the stage to the amp. By passing the output from a pickup through a potentiometer or 'pot' the player can control how much of the output reaches the amp.

The potentiometer might be seen as a very long piece of wire connected to the pickup at one end and the amp at the other. Any conductive material has a natural resistance to the flow of electricity so, if the wire were long enough, none of the signal would reach the amp. If the wire were shortened, some of the output would reach the amp but would pass only a weak signal. If the wire were shortened yet again, even more of the signal would reach the amp.

The volume control works by altering the resistance of a carbon or conductive plastic track from a pre-set value, 250 or 500k (kilohms) up to literally infinity. By turning the pot to the right the resistance is decreased so more of the guitar signal can pass so the guitar gets louder at the amp.

A pot in real life!

Fitting a new pot

If you change the pickups on your guitar from single coil to humbucker you'll need to fit a new pot to suit the increased output of the pickup. Single coil pickups usually need a 250k audio taper pot. Humbucking pickups need a 500k audio taper pot.

Fitting a new pot is very simple. All you need is a soldering iron and a pair of small cutters to remove the old pot. Remember to draw a picture of the connections and label the wires before snipping. Strip and tin the wires then solder to the new pot.

Many manufacturers now use a small value (.001mf or similar) capacitor between the input and output connections of the volume control. This allows treble to pass through the capacitor, bypassing the effects of the

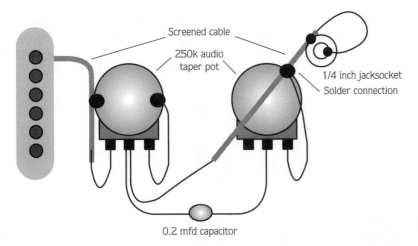

Screened cable

250k audio
taper pot

1/4 inch jacksocket

Solder connection

0.2 mfd capacitor

Basic guitar circuitry

volume control to compensate for loss of highs when the guitar is turned down. This is a simple and highly effective modification to make.

Tone control

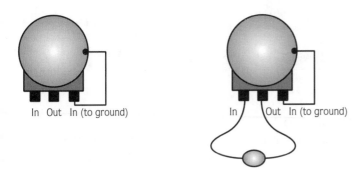

In   Out   In (to ground)

In   Out   In (to ground)

Left: Guitar volume control potentiometer
Right: Capacitor fitted to volume control to give more treble at low volumes

The tone control is another pot connected to an added extra. A low value capacitor is added before the input of the tone control allowing nothing but the bass frequencies to pass through. While the volume control is wired to provide no resistance when turned fully 'on' the tone control is wired to provide maximum resistance between the hot connection and the ground when turned full 'on'. As the control is turned 'down' the resistance between ground and hot gradually decreases enabling more and more of the treble frequencies to pass through and disappear.

By adjusting the value of the capacitor the character of the guitar can be set to suit yourself. A switch enabling various capacitor values can easily be made for custom guitar sounds. Commercial manufacturers use either .02 or .05 value capacitors. Higher capacitor values enable more treble to pass through for a deeper tone. Use .02 capacitors for a single coil pickup, .05 capacitor for a humbucker.

Pickup selector

Selecting pickups or combinations provides a quick and effective way of changing the sound you get from your guitar. 'Three position' switches are used, but five position types are now the most common and most popular method of pickup selection on Stratocaster guitars.

Gibson and other 'Standard' guitars use a three position selector switch

A vintage Stratocaster has a three position lever switch

A five position selector switch is now standard on the Fender Stratocaster.

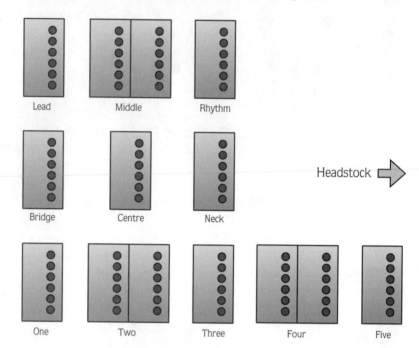

Pickup coil split/coil tap

One coil of a dual-coil humbucker pickup can be switched off if the manufacturer provides three 'hot' wires and a ground lead from the pickup. This enables the player to have a single coil sound from a humbucking pickup.

Some humbucking and single coil pickups are wound with a 'tap'. This is simply a second 'hot' wire connected to a point halfway along the coil. If this wire is selected, the pickup will appear brighter with less output than the full coil.

Phase switch

Phase switches take advantage of the way in which positive and negative voltages are created when the string moves towards and away from the magnets. If both magnets show the same pole to the strings (north – north) the push pull effect creates voltages travelling in the same direction at the same time.

If one of the magnets is reversed to show north – south instead, then the push will produce a positive charge in one coil and a negative charge in the other coil. These two waves partially cancel each other out and an 'out of phase' tone is produced. It would be impossible to physically take the magnet out every time you wanted this effect so by reversing the status of the 'hot' and 'ground' wires a similar effect is produced.

Pickup phase/tap/split switches can be incorporated into 'push pull' pots, or fitted as additional switches on the guitar body. Recently this method has been unpopular with manufacturers as additional switches add to the cost. Stratocaster guitars are perfect for pickup experiments as the plastic scratchplate is easily worked to include additional switches. Of course if you decide you don't like your modifications then simply buy another scratchplate. It's a lot easier than filling and refinishing a high gloss Les Paul!

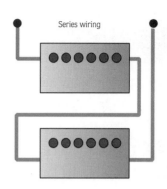

Series/parallel wiring

Humbucking pickups can be wired in series or parallel configurations. In series the signal from one coil passes through the next, in parallel both conductors of both pickups are connected to the output.

The tonal advantages of either series/parallel wiring are in the ears of the listener. Historically series came first with parallel being a modification. Gibson pickups are series wired, although any four conductor pickup can be switched for parallel wiring or hardwired either way. To my ears the series sound is a better one.

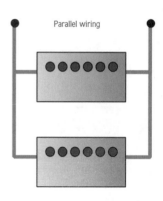

Series and parallel wiring of pickups

Active and passive electronics

A guitar has 'passive' electronics if no energy source other than the pickups is required. An ordinary guitar with two or three pickups, tone and volume controls uses a passive circuit. In this case the tone and volume controls simply attenuate the current from the pickup by dissipating all or part of the signal to ground.

If a guitar uses an internal pre-amp to boost the signal before it leaves the instrument then the electronics are called 'active' and require some power source, usually a 9V battery, to power them. The active circuitry gives the player more control over the tone of the guitar, adding certain frequencies instead of simply subtracting from the guitar signal.

Active electronics were very popular during the eighties but the need for maintenance (guitarists hate batteries in guitars!) meant that active guitars never became the standard.

Hybrid active guitars which use battery powered electronics for just one special feature are now appearing. The Jackson PC1 Phil Collen guitar has special active electronics which can be switched in or out of the regular circuitry. Jackson fit a Floyd Rose Sustainer system to the PC1 which needs a rather hefty 18V DC power supply from two 9V batteries in special compartments.

Active electronics are more usually fitted to bass guitars where on board pre-amp and EQ is a popular option. For example; six of the seven basses in the current Washburn catalogue have active electronics as standard. Precise control over tone and volume is important for bass players who need to be present in a mix without being too obvious. Acoustic/electric guitars very often have on board pre-amp and graphic for the same reason.

The 'power on' switch for the battery is concealed inside the jack socket on an active guitar. This means that to avoid draining the battery you must remember to unplug the guitar each time you put it down. It's the same for your guitar effects pedals too which have the battery connector wired to the input socket, usually on the right of the pedal.

5

Guitar accessories

So what? You thought that you could buy a guitar and that's it? You'll need a few other bits to go along with your new purchase, some now – some later on.

Riff-o-matic
If you regularly learn solos from tape or record you often need to listen to parts of the recorded solo very carefully, sometimes you might even wish that you could hear the solo in isolation. Just for this job there is a brilliant invention called a 'phrase sampler' which is exactly that – a small sampler which enables you to play back guitar solos repeatedly. The phrase sampler can also slow the sample down or even make it clearer by killing the bass.

Tutor CD ROM and practice aids
Practice aids are big business, and with computers arriving in every home, software publishers haven't been slow to produce 'interactive' tutor material for sound and video lessons at your own pace. Ubisoft and eMedia are just two of the software firms that offer computer based guitar lessons on CD ROM. The quality of the software is usually good, although the argument remains as to whether a £40 CD ROM is a good substitute for three or four good guitar lessons. You also have to consider your ability to operate both the computer and the guitar at the same time, and your ability to get on with the material that the publisher has chosen. If you don't like the examples that your real live teacher is giving you, you can just ask him to try another approach. A CD ROM can't do that!

Gig bags, hard cases etc.
Stop! Don't even think about leaving the store without a gig bag or case. The cardboard box that your new guitar came is not going to last five seconds in the back of your car, you will jeopardise the resale value of your guitar and you will risk the safety of the guitar! Buy a gig-bag, hard case, semi-flight or flight case when you buy the guitar. And if you don't know the difference – read on.

Gig bags
Gig bags are always made of black nylon or other man made waterproof material and offer basic protection from scratches and knocks but not

Gig bags offer basic protection from scratches and knocks

from crushing or flexing damage. Depending on price they can be thin and lightweight offering little protection to the guitar. More expensive bags have more padding and large pockets for music books and other bits that players habitually carry around. Most bags have shoulder straps which should not be relied on as they have a habit of breaking. Use nylon cable ties to fasten the strap to the bag, you won't be removing the strap anyway in case you lose it.

Incidentally these bags can protect your guitar from plenty as I found out when my Les Paul fell from the back of my Jeep at 35mph. I watched the guitar land on its back and slide to the side of the road. Obviously I hastily stopped the car and rescued my prize guitar from the wheels of a passing lorry. The guitar was completely all right and still in tune!

* Use a gig bag when carrying your guitar with you from home to the car and to the gig.
* Never trust a gig bag to protect your guitar when it is out of your sight.
* Pros: Lightweight, anonymous, hands-free.
* Cons: Breaking straps, no neck support, no bracing.

Hard shell cases

Hard shell cases are often supplied with more expensive guitars such as Gibson or Fender. They are traditionally made from light ply or particle board covered in material and stitched together. Cases like these offer marginally more protection than gig bags, but the thin ply and design of the case offer very little protection against crushing if stood on for example. Some hard shell cases can be nearly as bulky as flightcases but offer nowhere near the same level of protection.

Hard shell cases waiting to be packed into the larger flightcase trunk for shipping

* Use a hard shell case if one is supplied with your guitar but don't expect it to last long in the back of the van.
* Pros: Status when supplied with expensive instrument.
* Cons: Can be heavy and not as anonymous as a gig bag.

Semi-flight cases

Semi-flight cases are similar to traditional hard-shell boxes but constructed of plastic or polycarbonate material rather than wood. These cases are lightweight compared to full flight cases but still offer the rigidity that a gig bag does not have. This is important if your guitar is particularly valuable and you may be in a situation where you don't want to risk a gig bag but haven't the space for a flight case. Inside the case the guitar is held firmly in a moulded tray which is fitted to the profile of the guitar. There's little room for accessories inside; there's usually a small space just behind the heel of the guitar, just large enough for a packet of strings. Semi-flight cases can also be locked and will protect the guitar from scratches, knocks, crushing and flexing damage, but they are unlikely to survive a major disaster.

The Westone Voyager moulded guitar case – pic courtesy FCN

* Use a hard shell case of your guitar is fragile or prone to neck damage.
* Pros: Almost lightweight, lockable, rigid construction means little chance of neck damage.
* Cons: Bulky compared to a gig bag. Little room for accessories. Can only be used for guitars of a similar shape. Associated with valuable instruments making a possible attraction for thieves.

Full flight cases

Full flight cases are custom made wooden and aluminium containers constructed from 5mm birch ply, often faced with an extremely tough 'diamond board' and edged in aluminium with steel 'butterfly' catches and hinges. These cases will protect your instrument from virtually any kind of attack, they are completely secure and almost impossible to make a quick getaway with on foot owing to their heavy weight.

The guitar lies in a moulded foam insert which is shaped to fit the profile of the guitar exactly. Accessories can be stored anywhere in the case where the foam is cut away as full flight cases are box shaped for easy stowage. As these kind of cases are very expensive, few guitarists go to the expense of ordering a custom made case for just one guitar. More often a trunk is made to hold many guitars for shipping (*pic left*).

Sometimes the guitar is simply zipped inside a gig bag and placed in the trunk. Contrary to some stories a full flight case is not pressurised or airtight but it will provide maximum protection for your instrument or equipment.

Full flight case equipment

* Use a full flight case if your guitar is often carried in the back of the van or even in another vehicle. If you plan any long term touring it's essential that as much of your equipment as possible is flightcased.
* Pros: Virtually indestructible, very flexible bulk storage, easy to pack.
* Cons: Very heavy, difficult to store when not travelling, inflexible if you have a custom made case.

Guitar stands and hangers

Buying yourself a guitar stand is the second most intelligent thing (after buying your guitar) that you will ever do. Even Hendrix put his guitar down from time to time. Trouble is that wherever you put it, someone wants to sit on it or trip over it.

A guitar stand is a lightweight frame made to stand on the floor and hold your guitar upright. Guitar stands come in many shapes and sizes from simple tube steel to large compartmentalised flightcases. Look for a stand with a heavy base and a good centre of balance. The best stands break down for carrying with your other accessories. You might want to wait a while before buying one so leaving your guitar on a bed or in its case (you did buy a case didn't you?) is OK.

Always use a guitar stand to hold your instrument whenever you put it down. If you use an amp and cab it's easy to make a guitar holder which sits under your amp and gives you something to rest your guitar in. Guitar hangers are a good solution if you want to keep your guitars at home and easy to get at when you want top play. It's easy to make your own if you don't want to buy but make sure the materials – and the wall are strong enough to hold at least 5 kilos of dead weight for an indefinite period of time.

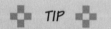

TIP

If you have to lean your guitar against something, put it face first. Then the guitar rests on the flat fingerboard while protecting the finish and controls of the front of the guitar. If someone knocks your guitar onto its face it is potentially a lot less damaging. You risk a few fret marks but it is a lot better than snapping off your headstock.

Picks

Picks, plectrums, flatpicks... Pretty much the same thing. All are small pieces of bone, plastic or pretty much anything that comes to mind held between the thumb and first finger and used to strike the string instead of your fingernail. Picks have been made of: plastic, nylon, tortoiseshell, bone, metal, glass and stone.

Anything small enough and hard enough can be used as a pick. I've been pressganged into guitar duties a few times with nothing but a 5p piece between me, shame and embarrassment. The 5p was great, pity about the playing. I'm constantly amazed by the amount of people who'll spend £1000's on new guitar to MIDI converters, multi-effects etc. in the search for new and exciting sounds. All of my greatest (and I mean sounds that made me *money*) sounds come from an unusual choice of plectrum. Try:

* A broken guitar string, held at 90 degrees to the guitar. Play the guitar with the windings of the broken string. The sound of the windings scraping against each other is great with a volume pedal and lashings of thick reverb.
* A 5p coin. I've got my own theories about this. I firmly believe that different currencies lend different sounds to the guitar. There must be a gag in here somewhere but I'm beggared if I can find it...
* A silver shilling (gawd bless yer sir...) makes a great sound. Brian May swears by this.
* A paper clip (or three) clipped onto the string so that it is free to move then rattle against the other strings when the guitar is strummed. Producers cannot figure out what the noise is...
* Thimbles on your first and second finger. Tap the wound strings lightly with the tips of the fingers for dulcimer type noises.
* A paintbrush makes a creepy sound.
* Play the guitar with a violin bow but avoid looking like an idiot at the same time.
* Lay the guitar on your knee and play with pencils or light paintbrushes held as drumsticks. You need to use an open tuning for this unless you have a hand growing out of your leg.

Capo

The capo is a metal or rigid plastic bar which is clamped across the fingerboard to relieve the barre finger. It's often used by 12 string guitarists who tune down one semitone to relieve pressure on the strings and so avoid breaking so many. Sometime the capo is used by electric guitarists, most notably Keith Richards who regularly uses a capo combined with open tunings. 'Tumbling Dice' for instance is a E open tuning with a capo at the seventh fret. If you are looking for inspiration simply adding a capo at the third fret and using open shapes often brings on new ideas. Capos come in many shapes and prices.

Wrap around capo – pic courtesy FCN

The most successful are 'Shubb' type lever capos which can be removed with one hand. Capos with elastic straps give up after a few weeks when the elastic loses its ability to keep the bar on the fingerboard.

Don't overlook the capo as a real aid to songwriting. Capos on stage can be a problem if your guitar has a high action as sometimes you will need to retune when the capo is in place. Install the capo on a spare guitar before you go on or make room in the set for a quick tune-up.

Leads and cables

OK you have a great guitar, great rack effects and a towering amp. But when you stand on your distortion pedal all you get is crackle and hiss. Somewhere your sound is disappearing into the ether. Stop. Before you drag out your credit card again, look at your leads.

Fact. Nine out of ten guitar sound problems are caused directly by your guitar lead. Change your guitar lead first and those problems usually disappear. Guitar leads simply don't last forever. The copper conductors inside the cable will over time oxidise (rust) leading to increased resistance. The constant motion of the cable produces stress inside the cable and at each end, eventually the conductors will break.

The input of your amp needs all it can get to give you the best sound or it's like having fluff on your needle. Turn the record player up all you want, you just get more noise. To make matters worse, some players use curly cable! Aggghhh! Curly cables are the Devil's work. Put on earth to curse lowly guitar techs who get bawled out at the end of the gig. Do yourself a favour:

1 Carefully wrap all your curly guitar leads.
2 Put them in a carrier bag.
3 Throw the carrier bag in the bin.

Choosing a guitar lead is simple. Discard anything curly or in a bright colour. Black is the only colour for guitar leads unless you want to look like the window of Toys 'r Us. Avoid any lead with a moulded plug. Go for the leads with metal barrel plugs that come apart and reveal the connections inside. Eventually that connection will break.

Look at the strain relief. The best Neutrik plugs have strain relief that does not clamp or bend the cable. The best strain relief of all actually allows a bit of give as the cable twists in the plug. Avoid 'No Squawk' or 'Quiet Connection' plugs. These have small pins which disconnect the 'hot' tip from the cable connection when you unplug the guitar. Ultimately this gadget will fail and you will have to replace the plug.

Look out for manufacturers like Klotz, Whirlwind and DiMarzio for the best cable. Guitar cables are rarely blessed with major artist endorsements but if you really want to go the whole distance try a limited edition Steve Vai Artist guitar cable!

 **INFO**

Hot wire and hot connections don't actually mean that the cable is hot. Hot is a name used when identifying the inner core of the cable. In three core balanced cable only one of the two inner connections is 'hot'. In guitar cable only the single inner core is 'hot'. Unless your amp is dangerously faulty you won't get an electric shock if you touch the 'hot' tip of a live jack. All you'll hear is a loud buzz as you temporarily turn your body into a very poor radio receiver.

Practice amps

A practice amp is a small amp – 5 to 10 watts output with a headphone socket and a distortion circuit built in. Some neat models also have plug in connections for your Hi Fi or Walkman for playing along. Extra neat models have all this and built in reverb. A practice amp is used when you want to play along in your dressing room or bedroom or warm up before a show. In general practice amps aren't used for gigging because they don't have enough output. However a good practice amp can be excellent in a recording situation as they can be driven hard at low volumes.

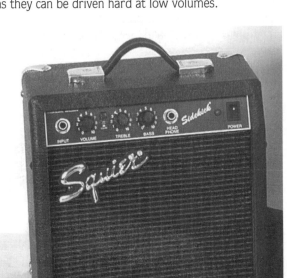

The Squier Sidekick®
practice amp (pic courtesy
Arbiter)

If you are on a budget you may have to decide whether to buy an amp or a multi-effects to practise with. The answer is that no guitar player becomes great on his or her own. A multi-effects might have 200 sounds but you can't plug your best friend into it when you want to practise your songs. Every practise amp has a distortion channel, just a little more money gets a Walkman socket and some reverb. So buy an amp and play with your mates and leave the button pushing to the keyboard player.

Straps

Like anything you wear, your guitar strap says a lot about you. My personal preference is for a plain black strap. That's because I generally wear black on stage and I like my guitar to be the centre of attention. Some players like straps with tassels and fringing, some players like straps with pockets for picks. Some even have their names embroidered on their strap.

Straplocks

There is *nothing* more embarrassing than feeling your guitar slip from under your arm in the middle of a show. However the embarrassment soon turns to angst when you survey the damage. It's very rare for a guitar strap to physically break, more common for the strap to be twisted over the strap button. The solution to this is to use a straplock.

There are several different sorts of straplock from 'Gripper Buttons' (outsize strap buttons) through to plastic discs and metal fixings that physically lock the strap to a special strap button. If you are on a budget then simply drive the strap button screw through the material of the strap but be careful and test that the material isn't thinner than the leather hangers.

Replacement bridge

The guitar bridge is one of the only two points on your guitar where the strings meet the body, and it's critical that any replacement fitting is chosen correctly. Choose a bridge replacement if your present bridge is so corroded that adjustment is impossible or if the bridge isn't providing as much functionality as you'd like – it may not be a tremolo model or you might want the additional sound of a piezo electric bridge.

Fitting a tremolo bridge to a non tremolo body involves serious routing of the guitar body and is the kind of thing that you just can't do with a chisel and a kitchen table. Treat re-routing a guitar body as refinishing an old guitar. It's unlikely you'll be able to sell it again and you might find trading your present guitar against a model with a factory fitted tremolo is a better bet. If routing is the way ahead for you I would take the stripped body to your local cabinet maker and pay them to do the job right.

Tremolo stop bar tailpiece attachments are now available as replacements for Les Paul guitars although a Bigsby style 'surface mounted' tremolo arm which doesn't require routing is probably a better option.

Replacement scratchplate

Next to a replacement bridge the most popular refit for your guitar is the scratchplate. The best bit about fitting a new scratchplate is that it can usually be done in a couple of hours with the minimum of tools and looks

Blood curdling scratchplate from Mega Designs

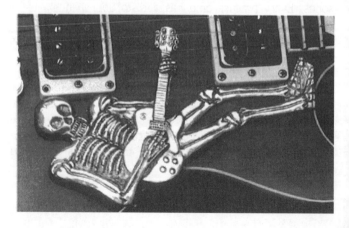

great. Mighty Mite and DiMarzio make replacement scratchplates in all kinds of materials and finishes. More recently an English maker 'Mega Designs' of Cricklewood, London was offering scratchplates in Pewter with outrageous designs along a Gothic/Heavy Metal theme.

Special effects

Wow. Big subject and worth a book or two on its own. I bought my first guitar effects pedal (an Electro Harmonix Small Stone phaser) before I bought my first guitar. I've always loved effects. Since my Small Stone days guitar effects have moved on some. I started working in studios when the height of sophistication was a Great British Spring. This was the reverb for the studio, literally a drainpipe with a few long springs down the middle of it. The spring reverb was a mechanical device which used voltage controlled analogue circuitry. During the sixties and seventies guitarists could only buy 'analogue' effects which sounded great but could only add or take away from the sound of the guitar, they couldn't add cathedral style reverb or turn the guitar into a piano. Something had to change.

In the early eighties the effect world was turned on its head by the groundbreaking Boss DD-5 Digital Delay. This was the first affordable guitar effects pedal to use digital circuitry. Up until this point digital tools were out of reach of the ordinary guitarists, frustrating at a time when digital sampling was new and exciting. The DD-5 brought digital effects to the guitarists feet for the very first time.

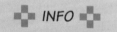

INFO

The trend for retro gear has made those old unwanted analogue pedals into collector's items!

Definition

A guitar effect is usually a small battery powered foot pedal or bank of pedals. Professional effects with more features are often cased in a 19 inch rack with a remote footswitch. It's called an effect (short for special effects) because its job is to add a special effect to the 'plain vanilla' guitar sound. Any guitarist can use effects and any guitar can be effected. Electric guitars are simple to connect as the effect can simply be placed in line from the guitar to the amp. Electric / Acoustic guitars are just as easy if the guitar has a jack socket. Even normal acoustic guitars can be effected by adding the effect to the microphone sound passing through any mixing desk Sometimes an effected sound is called the 'wet' sound and the normal sound is called the 'dry' sound.

Guitar effects come in two formats; The 'stomp box' and the 'multi-effect'. These two formats both offer their own advantages and disadvantages and choosing which format will suit you best is a little like deciding on whether to buy hi fi 'separates' or a 'MIDI' system.

'Stomp Box'

Foot pedals are sometimes called 'stomp boxes' because the effect is turned on and off by a footswitch on top of the pedal. All foot pedals just have one or maybe two similar effects and are generally cheaper to buy than multi-effects. All the controls are on the pedal including the footswitch. The pedal is normally powered by either a 9 V battery or an external power supply.

* Pros: Easily replaceable; if one effect is bad then replace it with another without losing your whole sound. Usually tougher than multi-effects and the effect is often higher quality as the manufacturer doesn't have to cram so much into such as small package.
* Cons: Usually only one effect for your money so can be expensive to gather a good collection of effects. Battery often fades too soon and the pedal needs to be unplugged when not in use. Controls are on the floor and difficult to adjust mid gig.

Typical Stomp Box – The revolutionary Boss DD-5 meant digital effects for the common man

Multi-effects

The main advantage of multi-effects is that all your effects are available from one package so there's no messing around with rat's nests of leads and batteries pre-gig. They can be in the foot pedal style, or rack mounted with optional foot pedal. Effects can be brought together in varying combinations (patches) to create sounds which can be stored (programs) and brought back at the push of a button. MIDI multi-effects can be linked to other devices making the whole of your effects automatic. You may not even need to push a footswitch to change sounds. Multi-effects are always powered by a mains adapter.

Boss ME-30 multi-effects unit puts all your effects into one easy to use unit

* Pros: All your effects in one place and all your sounds saved as patches to be easily brought up during the gig. No interconnecting leads or batteries. Rack mounted multi-effects have controls which can easily be reached during a gig without having to bend down.

> * Cons: All your sounds in one place? What happens if your multi-effect pedal goes down? Often the effects are lower quality, especially if it is a budget effect. Expensive optional footswitching. Complex menus mean lots of programming for even simple sounds. Many players find that multi-effects are not reactive enough in a gig where you often want to make very quick adjustments or try out new things.

Some manufacturers offer polypropylene and plastic carrying cases to house your collections of stomp boxes. These are not strictly multi-effects but aim to offer the advantages of having all your pedals in the same place at the same time while protecting them during transit but without the programming and flexibility problems of multi-effects.

Boss BCB-6 carrying case for Boss effects

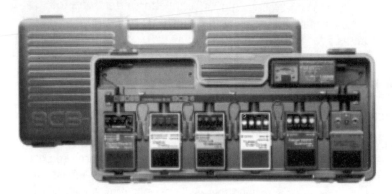

You'll still have to buy a power supply unless you want to spend all your gig money on batteries, and there are all those connecting leads to consider too. Boss have their ME-X which enables the user to add any combination of up three stomp box effects to the ME-X on board digital reverb and delays. Carrying cases also include on-board power transformers, remote switching and bypass functions to add multi-effects functionality to your stomp box effects collection.

Which is best?: Multi-effect or stomp box

Without question stomp boxes do have the edge on multi-effects. More players adopt multi-effects in the short term and then get bored and move on. The effects themselves can be over the top, distracting from the song and your technique, while they drive the rest of the band bananas. And who needs to be fiddling with menus while you should be concentrating on playing the guitar?

Caught by the fuzz

Everybody needs fuzz. Guitarists love fuzz because with a fuzz or distortion pedal we can turn the sweet sound of a vibrating string into something much more exciting. Fuzz and distortion effects chop the top and

Original guitar signal

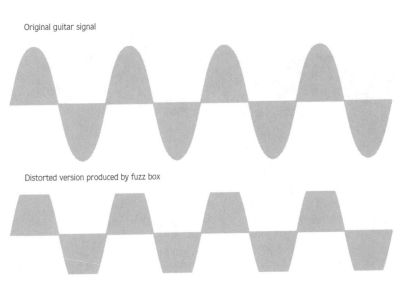

Distorted version produced by fuzz box

Distortion effect chops top and bottom from a sine wave to produce distortion

bottom off the waveform making the sound much harder, like a square wave produced by a synth. At the same time the fuzz pedal makes the guitar much more sensitive and boosts the amp input making it work harder to produce even more distortion.

There are so many fuzz pedals around, it's difficult to believe that fuzz and distortion wasn't available in foot pedal form until the early 1960's. Before then guitarists would create a distorting sound by razoring the cardboard speaker cone to make it rasp! At this time transistorised effects pedals were still experimental and expensively made to order by engineers like Jimi Hendrix guitar effects guru Roger Mayer.

Advancements in technology brought cheaper components, and in 1965 UK maker Macari designed their first commercial fuzz pedals. At the same time fuzz sounds started to appear on UK records, such as the PJ Proby single 'Hold Me', which included the first fuzz effect on a number one record. Macaris introduced the Coloursound range in the late sixties.

Throughout the Seventies the fuzz effect market was dominated by US pedals such as the Electro Harmonix 'Big Muff' and Arbiter Fuzz Face. In the early eighties the effect began to fall out of fashion, and players drifted away from the harsh transistorised distortion sound towards cheaper and more robust valve amplification. Recently the popular retro movement has prompted the reissue of some pedals including authentic replicas of vintage UK models such as the original Tonebender Mk2.

Guitar foot pedal effects

Amp simulators and pre-amps

An amp simulator aims to provide you with a way of getting loads of great amp sounds without carrying loads of great amps around with you. So you might want a Vox, a Marshall JCM900, a Boogie Dual Rectifier and a Fender Champ for just one show. Without an amp simulator that is

Roland GP-100 guitar amp
simulator

a good deal of expensive hardware to be carrying around. Digital amp simulators like the Yamaha DG1000 enable you to use the sounds of a large number of different amps.

The amp simulator looks like a cross between a pre-amp and a multi-effects unit. The sounds are stored as numbers but the amp simulator also has conventional front panel controls for tone, presence, distortion etc. Hundreds of amp sounds can be programmed in rehearsal then stored for you to recall with a footswitch or even by MIDI controllers. Amp simulators offer the benefits of many different sounds but must be connected to an amp or mixing desk for live use.

Other pre-amp rack units such as the Marshall 9004 are used in combination with a dedicated high powered amp such as a Peavey Classic 50/50 or Marshall 9200. In this case the pre-amp replaces the traditional front panel of the amplifier. The pre-amp has easily identifiable controls for volume, tone, presence etc. but doesn't have facilities for saving or recalling sounds. Many players prefer this type of pre-amp as small variations in tone and volume are often necessary while on stage.

An amp simulator is a pre-amp, that is it comes before the main power amp in any rig. The pre-amp does not have enough power to drive a speaker. However it's not a multi-effect. The multi-effect has many different guitar effects such as reverb, delay, distortion etc. The amp simulator usually doesn't have any of these, although some units such as the Roland GR100 combine conventional multi-effects with digital modelling circuitry which closely emulate the sound of many different amplifiers. The GR100 enables the guitarist to store all the sounds for a live set in just one piece of equipment.

Other pre-amps come in pedal form. These look like large floor effects pedals and can be used to boost the sound of a conventional amplifier. Foot pedal units such as the Mesa Boogie V Twin include a tube amplifier for natural distortion.

Power attenuator

The sound of a high powered tube amp has qualities which are impossible to emulate with microprocessor technology. However, this can cause a problem with sound levels when recording in a small studio or control room. In this case a device called a power attenuator may be inserted between the amp and speaker cabinet to control the amount of voltage that reaches the speakers. This enables the player to use a high output amp head without having to allow for the restrictions of the studio envi-

Marshall Powerbrake power
attenuator

ronment. A volume control is used to control how much volume comes from the speaker while the power attenuator soaks up the unwanted current.

Speaker emulator

Speaker emulators imitate the sound of a speaker cabinet. They are used in combination with a pre-amp when use of a conventional amp is impossible, or sometimes together with a speaker cabinet to allow the producer or engineer a choice of tones. The speaker emulator is not a power attenuator as it is not designed to be connected to the higher voltage speaker outputs of a conventional amplifier. Many multi-effects and amp simulators have a speaker emulator built in, making the purchase of additional units unnecessary. This is one way that a multi-effect can save you money.

Time based effects

Digital delay

A digital delay pedal uses sampling technology to produce an echo effect. The effect is digitally produced which gives an accurate echo image at the expense of the natural sound of an analogue device. At the input of the pedal the guitar sound is sampled at around 44.1khz (just over 440,000 times a second) The sampler looks at the waveform coming into the pedal and simply remembers the shape of the wave as a set of numbers. Then all it has to do is reproduce that same set of numbers as voltages, all the little voltages put together create another waveform which can be as far behind the original as the DSP (digital signal processor) has the memory to remember it.

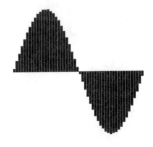

In a sampled sine wave the waveform is effectively 'photographed' 440,000 times per second (there are fewer samples in this illustration to aid clarity)

To save memory the computer might decide to ignore frequencies over and under a pre-set level. In this way the effect can appear much cleaner, but for some players it's the missing 'invisible' sounds which hold the true character of their instrument. Delay and echo are excellent tools for vibing up a guitar part by adding rhythmic echoes or for making a guitar solo seem to last longer as the repeats fade away.

The Boss Super Phaser

Echo

Echo is when part of the guitar sound is delayed as before but released later and the delayed part is repeated over and over to create a very familiar echo effect. Long ago this used to be made by messing with a tape recorder. Now things are much easier and tape recorders are more expensive so we can't mess with them any more.

Loops aren't something you find in a packet of breakfast food. A loop is a rhythm part which plays endlessly underneath a vocal or instrumental part. Many records use loops recycled from records made years or decades before the new parts were added. Loops are now samples created by music computers. Before samplers were invented the same effect was produced by using long loops of endless tape. So they were called 'tape loops', and now just 'loops'.

Aural exciter

An equalisation device with a sweep centre and gain control. Aural exciters process the sound by sending the lower frequencies to the speaker fractionally later than the treble frequencies. This enables the speaker to handle the sound more efficiently and produces a much clearer sound. The effect is to bring the guitar out in the mix without adding gain and to make the guitar sound a bit brighter than usual.

Phasing

Cool sixties psychedelic effect made famous by Jimi Hendrix. A phaser will take your guitar signal and delay a portion of it very slightly before mixing the delayed portion back into the output. The resulting phase cancellation produces the illusion of your guitar drifting in and out of the mix in a very pleasing fashion.

Set your phaser to slow and use anytime you need to drop back or 'pad' behind a vocal. Use a phaser in front of a high gain distortion pedal for Prince style solos with extra bite. Faster rate of phase adds a warbling shimmering sound which makes a good impression of a tremolo pedal. A stereo phaser splits the signal at the output providing a dry and effected signal or a phaser which 'pans' across from right to left.

Flanging

This is the famous 'jet aeroplane' sound, a close relation of the phaser but with a slightly different technique to produce a stronger effect. Flanging is best used after a high gain distortion during a strong rhythm part when it can really lift a rock chorus. Another popular flanging trick is to use a professional studio flanging device and stick the whole mix through it just once in the song at a key moment such as a half bar break between solo and verse.

Tremolo

REM bought the tremolo bang up to date in 1996. Tremolo is the effect that makes your guitar-ah-ah-ah sound like someone is turning the volume up and down all the time. Very cool with retro sixties bands and country musicians. Jim Dunlop makes a very good stereo tremolo.

Distortion effects

Fuzz

Once the poor man's valve tone, fuzz effects have a synthetic character of their own completely different to distortion or overdrive. Fuzz pedals such as the Coloursound Tonebender and Lovetone Big Cheese produce a thick square wave with very few overtones. Because of the enormous amount of gain that's introduced to the signal most people find that fuzz is best with single coil pickups because they actually work better with a weaker signal – a powerful pickup sound just turns to gritty mush. Don't buy a fuzz if you are looking for an overdriven tube amp sound. Do buy a fuzz if you want to make show stopping strange guitar noises.

Danelectro fifties inspired and highly individual 'Daddy O' fuzz pedal

Overdrive

Mild distortion sound used mainly for rhythm. This effect doesn't add enough gain to the guitar signal for the sound to sustain as long as most players like for soloing. Overdrive pedals should be used if you want to simulate the sound of an overdriven tube amp.

Distortion

Distortion is another overdrive effect with a slightly higher gain for blues soloing and heavy rhythm. Often combined with a high gain setting on the same pedal for more flexibility. More gain for solos but not enough for Steve Vai/Malmsteen shredding. Thick enough to be useful for pads.

High gain or metal

The principal effect for guitarists. High gain distortion turns the smooth sine wave of the guitar into a much harder square wave. This has the dual effect of making quiet sounds much louder while compressing louder sounds. The combined effect of all this is to instantly make the guitar feel much more exciting and expressive to play. Soloists particularly like this effect as complex parts which involve many light taps and touches are much easier to produce as the guitar pickups become super sensitive. Power chords suffer slightly as the distortion effect compresses each

The Boss HM-3 high gain distortion effects pedal

chord into a dense sound in which individual notes are very difficult to pick out. This characteristic is exploited by 'death metal' bands such as Sepultura or Metallica who compress the guitar sound and remove most of the mid range frequencies to produce their trademark 'scooped' sound.

Other names for distortion units include Hyper Fuzz, Turbo Distortion, Blues Driver, Blues Master, Guvnor, Shred Master.

Compression and EQ

Compression

It's easiest to think of a compressor as an automatic volume control squeezing your sound as you play. If you play a quiet passage the compressor lifts the volume slightly. During sudden loud notes or passages the compressor prevents any harsh electronic 'clipping' by reducing the output of the pedal. So the compressor helps your other effects by making the guitar a little easier to deal with, it can really help if you have a chorus or phaser pedal by smoothing and thickening chords. Strat and Telecaster players often add a compressor to their effects rack to add even more attack to their sound. The compression effect isn't very spectacular but the experienced player knows how important it is to use a compressor for good gain structure. Really skilful use of compression is invisible, all anyone should notice is more power and tone than they expected.

Limiter

Similar to a compressor, this acts to stop the volume of your guitar distorting an amp or mixing desk by limiting the output to a pre-set level. Useful for recording or if you like to play very hard without overdriving your amp. Very useful for bass guitar.

Equalisation (EQ)

This Dod graphic equaliser has many faders, each covering just a part of the frequency band (pic courtesy Arbiter)

Graphic EQ

This is the term used for devices which have many small vertical faders on the front or top of the box. Each control boosts or cuts the sound of just one frequency band. Graphic EQ is used when you want accurate control

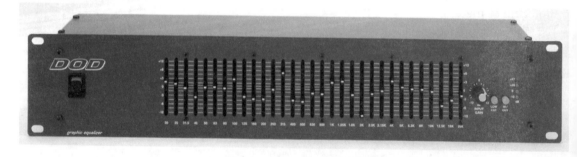

over just one small area of your sound without affecting any other fre-quencies. Because of this accuracy, graphic EQ is used by live sound engi-neers, bass players and acoustic guitarists! Typical uses include 'notching out' troublesome resonant frequencies from an acoustic/electric guitar, or removing hiss without losing presence.

Parametric EQ

This enables the engineer to select a broader range of frequencies which may be cut or boosted. This kind of EQ is found on mixing desks when having a fader for each EQ band would be impossible.

Wah-wah

A wah-wah pedal contains a pedal operated rotary potentiometer connect-ed to a parametric tone control. When the player moves the pedal, the rotary control sweeps over a pre-set range of frequencies which are boosted by the tone circuit. In this way the sound of the guitar appears to take on a vocal nature with the boosted mid range tones providing a filter effect.

The Boss GE-7 graphic equaliser is an example of the stomp box type

Because the pedal is foot operated, the wah-wah is very easy to use, the 'toe down' action is second nature to all musicians, and when com-bined with a funky guitar part, the Wah gives the guitar a percussive momentum that suits rhythm and blues, jazz and funk like nothing else. This effect is so attractive that keyboard, synth and even horn players have adopted the wah-wah.

One particularly good trick is to find a 'sweet spot' in the travel of the pedal that really suits your lead sound. Then jam in a drum stick or even tape the pedal up to add a midrange boost to your guitar solos. Prince uses this sound all the time. Alternatively, wah-wah and heavy phase sound very psychedelic together. Buy a Cry Baby if possible.

Auto wah

Auto-wah (spit-wah) is an effect that aims to automatically emulate the sound of the wah-wah pedal without the player having to move his or her foot (as if!). The pedal senses how loud the signal coming into the pedal is and adjusts the boosted frequency accordingly. So if you play a loud note the pedal sounds very sharp, if you play softly the pedal sounds deeper. This is OK for guitar solos but auto-wah really lacks the rhythm of the foot pedal and is not as popular.

Digital effects

Harmonist

Depending on your point of view this is either the best thing that every happened to you, or the one effect that is guaranteed to make everyone in the audience want to tear you to pieces. Essentially a tool which synthe-sises a note in harmony with the one you are playing, you can now merri-ly duet away with yourself as if there were two or even three guitar players on stage with you.

'Intelligent' or 'non intelligent' harmonisers are available, depending on your budget. The intelligent sort will harmonise accurately with your playing even when you are playing across modes or in minor keys. You usually have to give them a few clues first by selecting a time signature or such but some super intelligent types don't even need this. Non intelligent harmonisers are getting scarcer now but simply harmonise mathematically leading to the occasional wrong note.

Digitech 'whammy'.

A wah-wah style fabulous effect which changes the pitch of your guitar in real time (i.e. as you are playing it) when you move the rocker pedal. The effect is a little like having a very large locking tremolo system at your feet. It's ace for soloing along while using your foot to digitally bend the guitar note or notes up or down two or three octaves. Brilliant for rock soloing which traditionally espouses taste for mere spectacle. In the hands of goddess Jennifer Batten it's an awesome and frightening tool.

Octaver

A relation of the harmoniser but much simpler and possibly more effective, this kind of pedal simply produces a note on octave (twelve frets) above or below whichever guitar note you play into it. It only works on single notes but is really effective on solos when it produces earth shaking bass. Also useful for doubling bass lines during verses.

Pitch shifter

A little like an octaver but not restricted to octaves. It can produce any note in the scale in time with your guitar note. Half way between an octaver and harmoniser, it won't harmonise scales accurately enough but is useful for short passages.

Bass synth

A bass synth will synthesise a bass under your guitar with filter and attack properties. The resulting 'owww...' and 'aoiooo...' sounds are great for funk. Useful if your bass player goes AWOL, but could be seen as treading on the keyboard player's toes.

Utilities

Line selector

Sometimes called an A/B box, this isn't really an effect. Imagine you have maybe two amps which each have a great sound of their own and you want to use both on stage. You need an A/B box to switch cleanly between them. Connect your guitar to the input of the selector and the two outputs one to each amp.

So if your Valvestate is amp 1 and your Fender is amp 2, you can quickly change amps by just stomping on the footswitch. Turn upside down for two guitars into one amp.

Noise suppressor or noise gate

If you have a guitar which is noisy, or an effect which you love but which is too noisy between songs, you then cut the noise down with a noise suppressor. The noise gate acts in the opposite way to a compressor pedal by turning the output of the pedal right down (instead of up like a compressor) when the input level drops below a certain pre-set point. This works well if you use a high gain distortion pedal which produces a lot of noise when there's no signal going through the pedal to mask it. By inserting a noise gate between the high gain pedal and your amp you'll cut the unwanted noise and also help kill feedback.

Pre-amp

Not really an effect but more a device for boosting a low powered signal before it gets to your amp or mixing desk. If you own an expensive acoustic guitar and don't fancy putting a pickup in it, you might be using a piezo 'bug' on the bridge which will produce a very low output. In this case you would also use a preamp pedal in the signal chain before a graphic EQ pedal to shape that low powered signal into something your amp can use. Regular acoustic/electric guitars have preamp and EQ built in to save money and space

Just plain weird

Talk box

Produced most famously by Electro Harmonix in the early seventies but also by Heil and others, this is a pretty crude device. The talk box is just a small loudspeaker compression driver (of the type used in high end PA horns) inside a box with a couple of metres of plastic tubing.

By connecting the Talk Box to your guitar amp extension speaker socket the output of your amp goes up the tube and can be directed pretty much anywhere you like. Then if you put the end of the rubber tube in your mouth it's possible to shape words and sounds from the sound of your guitar coming through your amp and into the box.

The Talk Box is great for completely inimitable filter, wah and kazoo effects. The bad news is that if you want to use it live you have to have a mike and PA system handy or no-one else can hear the effect and also that the performer looks like someone undergoing dental surgery! Revolting? Certainly. Weird? Definitely.

Digitech Talker

Unsurprisingly, you may not find the idea of playing a show with three feet of rubber tubing hanging out of your mouth very attractive. For you and other sane but unadventurous types there are a couple of options. Firstly you could attach your guitar to a keyboard vocoder – fun but very expensive. Secondly you could use a Digitech Talker. Digital technology emulates the sound of those analog filters so you simply sing into a microphone and your guitar takes on the same envelope. Sing 'Ahhh!' and you

 INFO 

Most famously used 20 years ago in the celebrated 'Frampton Comes Alive' album by (surprisingly enough) Peter Frampton, and more recently adopted by LA rap musicians, the Talk Box may also loosen fillings with prolonged use. (The seventies were very good to those people at Electro Harmonix.)

guitar will sing 'Ahhh!' too, or seemingly anyway. It's a lot more fun than it sounds and certainly more hygenic. Think Daft Punk and Peter Frampton with a generous slice of P-Funk on the side. Yummy.

Valve effects

Another by product of the back-to-basics trend. The valve effect aims to combine the 'warmth' of the 'real tube valve sound' with the all the advantages of modern technology. These benefits also include the solid state transistor which incidentally was invented in 1947 to remove the world of troublesome valves.

Both valves and transistors have a similar function – to amplify a signal passing through. A glass valve or 'tube' is inefficient as it requires a high voltage to function and a lot of energy is lost and converted into heat. Transistors require much less voltage to perform, consequently a transistorised device is much smaller and can often be run from a single battery. However the waveform produced by a transistor is much harder than one produced by a valve which also reacts in a musical sense to the character of the signal passing through in a way that is impossible to emulate. So by marrying a valve based tone device to a transistor based power device manufacturers hope to be able to produce the best of both worlds.

The valve is popular with many players as they believe that valve devices have something to offer above transistors. In fact how much of the 'real valve sound' actually makes it into valve-solid state effects and amps is debatable.

Most of the high gain distortion sounds produced by low end 'valve' amps and effects are produced by silicon diode devices. The valves warm up the input stage but sure aren't doing all that high gain stuff on their own. If you are wondering whether to spend the extra on a valve based distortion device (particularly in the budget end of the market) do some intensive A/B comparisons before actually parting with that cash.

The Flip Valve distortion effect with 12AX7 valve

Rack effects

Multi-effects or dedicated effects processors can be rack mounted for protection and convenience. For the touring guitarist there is no other choice than to rack mount as much equipment as possible. Rack mounted equipment doesn't have to be packed and unpacked, the equipment can remain inside its protective case throughout the tour. The controls and front panels also remain undisturbed from one night to the next. As the guitar sounds can be programmed for the tour during rehearsals, or even during recording it's also much easier for the travelling guitarist to produce a consistently good sound.

Rack equipment can be divided into two sorts, guitar rack multi-effects and studio effects, both of which a guitarist may use on stage or in the studio.

Guitar rack multi-effects

Digital devices which produce every kind of traditional guitar effect and hundreds of complete pre-programmed guitar sounds which the player can swap between using a footswitch. The advantage of multi-effects is that the compact size enables the guitarist to travel with the minimum of equipment, although the multi-effect must still be connected to an external amplifier and speakers.

The Boss GX700 rack mounted multi-effects processor

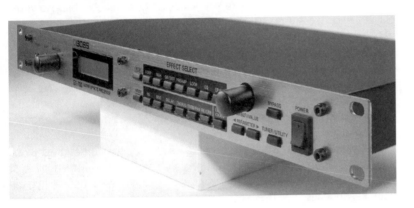

Studio effects

High end, very expensive studio equipment which has often been used during the making of the album before the tour. Studio equipment often simply does just one job so a guitarist using this kind of equipment must take more out on tour. Still, at this level the guitarist very rarely sets the gear up - so it's no problem. Studio effects are always rack mounted so can be easily transposed into a live situation with the addition of a pre-amp, power-amp, speakers and a flightcase.

In large venues the rack equipment provides a feed to the 'front of house' PA system as well as going directly to the speakers behind the guitarist. In this way the PA engineer can have almost total control over the guitarists sound from the audience. Any effect can be taken on the road like this, and it's common for high profile players to simply gather a selection of their favourite studio effects into a few flightcases and hook 'em up to an amp or two instead of using ready made guitar multi-effects. It's the same argument as stomp boxes versus multi-effects.

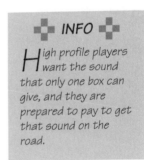

✦ *INFO* ✦

High profile players want the sound that only one box can give, and they are prepared to pay to get that sound on the road.

The Digitech 21122

Here's a good question ... how come my effects don't sound the same through my stack as they do through my headphones?
Multi-effects produce guitar sounds which are almost production ready, in other words all the reverb, chorus and compression that would normally be added after the guitar track is recorded is instead produced by the effects processor so you get an enormous and totally professional sound in isolation. This is why headphone effects are so popular, they really do use all the studio tricks to make you sound as good as possible. However players find that the multi-effects don't sound as good through an ordinary amp.

The issue is that most guitar amps are based on a 1940 design , itself based on an old radio! The amp is made to make the plain old guitar as big and loud as possible with big unresponsive speakers, crude and powerful valve amplification and an EQ system that's designed to boost the loud middle EQ frequencies, the same ones that the effects designers want to lose.

Many multi-effects have programmed sounds that are designed to be used through an amp but these are mainly conventional distortion/boost effects and don't include the enormous pad sounds that sound so huge in your headphones. For best results with these, use the PA system instead with a split feed from your guitar lead just before the amp.

If your effects don't sound so good through your amp, use the PA system instead with a split feed from your guitar lead just before the amp.

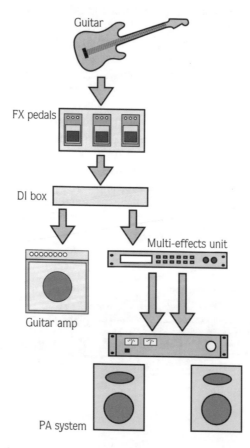

Put together your own guitar effects rack

The case

Rack cases can be made from almost any material you like with some considerations. Bear in mind that your finished case will need to be tough enough to protect your equipment while at the same time being light enough to carry into the car or van at the end of the evening. In many bands the rack cases often double as trolley, step, amp stand, bed, etc. so your case will have to protect your equipment from the rest of your band and the audience, as well as the usual road handling that it normally gets. Use only 5mm plywood for your case – particle (chip) board and MDF aren't suitable as both materials absorb water.

Handles and castors etc. can be purchased from Maplin or Strings & Things who carry the more expensive (but very reliable) Ernie Ball range of accessories. Choose a suitable height for your case in rack units and remember to add space for future equipment. If planned carefully your case might also have drawer space, computer and keyboard space or even space for a 1U light attachment.

TIP

Some plastic beer crates come in a convenient 19 inch size. Find yourself a couple, cut the bottle holders out and use self tapping screws to fix your effects to the frame! Instant rack!

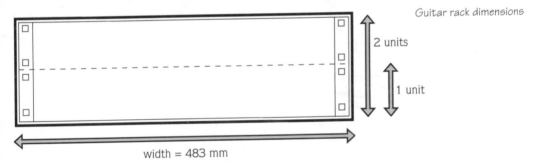

Guitar rack dimensions

2 units

1 unit

width = 483 mm

Rack equipment dimensions

Height in units	Width (mm)	Height (mm)	Depth
1U	483	44	305
2U	483	88	305
3U	483	132	305
4U	483	176	305
5U	483	220	305
6U	483	264	305
7U	483	308	305
8U	483	352	305

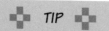

✤ TIP ✤

If you want my opinion, stick with a good quality combo and some high quality stomp boxes, at least until the point when somebody else gets the job of lifting your gear out of the venue at the end of the evening.

The gear

Using a rack of pre-amps, effects and an amp is a little like choosing hi-fi separates over a 'MIDI' living room stereo. You get to choose the bits you want, but it will be more expensive. One advantage of rack gear is that if you don't like or get bored with a particular part it's easy to replace it without ditching the whole thing. The downside is that putting the whole thing together is a lot more expensive and complicated than simply buying an amp and a load of effects.

Pre-amp

Don't put your guitar into your effects without a little tweaking first. Your guitar needs to be slightly boosted to match the input levels that the effects are expecting and any tone adjustments are usually done before the effects at this stage. A pre-amp essentially does the job of the front panel on a combo amp with controls for gain, presence and EQ etc. but without the power amp and speakers. Look for products such as the Marshall 9004 Stereo Pre-Amp or Yamaha DG-1000.

Effects including EQ and reverb

After the pre-amp you'll need your effects. These can be rack mounted professional multi-effects such as the Digitech GSP2101 or the Boss GR100. The other approach, and the one favoured by the real pros, is to simply cram a couple of flightcases with the same effects (or 'outboards') as your average run of the mill top flight rock and roll guitar hero would find in the kind of studios they would frequent. So you are looking at maybe £1,000 worth of Urei compressor, a couple of Lexicon reverbs, an Eventide harmoniser or two, certainly a Drawmer compressor etc.

Whatever you use, studio separates, multi-effects or both, you'll need to think about the order you'd like to chain them in, matching them for input and output levels and most importantly switching (see later in this chapter). The great advantage of multi-effects, and one which is sometimes overlooked, is that all your patching and switching is done in one press of your foot. The multi-effects knows that a particular configuration is held in a preset program and internally does all that complex wiring and rewiring in a second.

With separates it becomes much more difficult. The complex task of patching and footswitching is handled by a MIDI patchbay through which all the effects are channelled. This is programmed by the technician before the tour and either triggered by a footswitch or by another MIDI source such as the keyboard player or even a master computer switching the lighting rig, keyboard effects, guitar effects, etc. all at the same time.

Power amp

Same as the power amp in your combo but a lot louder and much higher quality. Some models have limited tone control but stereo volume controls are the norm. Good examples might be the Peavey/Classic 50/50 or Rocktron Velocity 500

Speakers

At this level, speaker systems usually arrive in flightcases with a couple of tons of power amp attached. Big names in this field are Mesa Boogie, Trace Elliot and Marshall. Speakers have to be weighted and balanced to match the power amp output and the local environment. It's not unheard of for guitarists to disconnect two or more cabs in a Quad stack if the on stage conditions aren't right.

Trace Elliott bass speaker system on stage

Acoustic multi-effects

Very often the acoustic guitar player gets a raw deal on stage where power and the ability to move lots of hair at high pressure often means the sensibility of a simple acoustic guitar gets lost. To redress the balance manufacturers have collected some useful tools together as acoustic-electric multi-effects. These don't have the 'special' effects such as multi-tap delays or distortion but concentrate instead on EQ, reverb and chorus effects, enabling the acoustic-electric guitar player to manage the sound of the acoustic guitar from on stage rather than leave it to the guy on the PA. The DOD Acoustic One, and Boss AD-5 are good examples. Any acoustic – electric guitar will work with a multi-effects unit, and some players even use acoustic guitar multi-effects to enhance the sound of their electric guitar.

INFO

Bass multi-effects are similar to acoustic multi-effects but with bass-centric tools such as compression and EQ.

Effects, analogue or digital?

Analogue means voltage controlled. Analogue effects produce a smooth sound with the dynamics of the guitar and player controlling the resulting sound of the effect. A digital effects processor must sample the sound many thousand times in every second before the samples can be manipulated by a computer to produce the sound of your guitar plus whatever effects the computer can produce as well.

Analogue and digital waveforms. Each one of these points is recorded as a number which is then used as a basis for computer calculations. More importantly, all the information between the points is lost

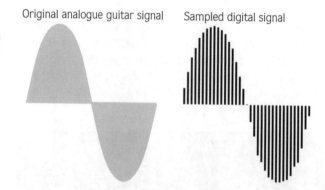

Original analogue guitar signal   Sampled digital signal

This process lends itself very well to reverbs and delays, when you don't want the sound of the guitar changed at all, just put into a different space. However many guitarists prefer a warmer sound as produced by the analogue effects processing the guitar sound. Some multi-effects now have a combination of effects, including analogue distortions and wah-wah but digital delays and reverbs. The jury is out on which sounds better, but if you want my opinion, see stomp boxes!

Chaining stomp boxes

If you have more than one stomp box you need to consider in which order the effects will be chained. This has as much influence on your sound as the effects themselves. A typical example (because it works so well) is the distortion and delay combination of pedals. For many players their distortion tone is as much a part of their sound as their guitar tone. If you use the distortion box before the delay box the delay will create echoes of each distorted note and the dynamics of each note, loud or soft etc. If you put the delay before the distortion the effect will be to distort the delays, instead of the other way around. So the way the effects are connected dictates the way they will actually sound.

Chaining stomp boxes

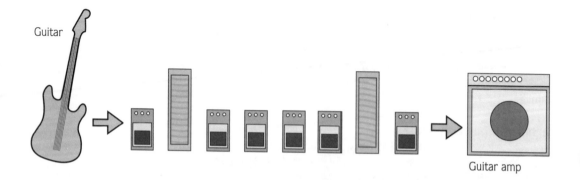

Guitar

Guitar amp

Connection order for stomp boxes

1	Compressor
2	Wah-wah
3	Overdrive or high gain distortion
4	Phaser
5	Flanger/chorus
6	Noise gate
7	Volume
8	Delay/reverb

Stage 1: Guitar to compressor and wah

Any dynamic pedals that you have should go at the start of the chain. wah, octave, compressor, etc. anything that relies on the shape (waveform) of the note to produce its effect. The compressor will boost the output of your single coil pickups and add attack to each note. This doesn't work nearly as well for high output humbucking pickups.

Stage 2: Wah to distortion.

Now the shape of the guitar note is being amplified and effected by the dynamic pedals and further shaped to fit neatly into your distortion effects. All distortion effects smooth the waveform by clipping the top and bottom of the wave.

Stage 3: Distortion to modulation

Modulation effects which colour the sound such as chorus, flanger and phasing usually add noise so insert them here after the distortion. The best guitar sounds are those which come out you out of the blue, having noise in the way just warns you that something is about to happen which spoils the surprise. The noise gate will kill any residual noise that the effects produce. Any 'too bad' noise can also be killed by the volume pedal in an emergency.

Stage 4: Volume and decay

Delay works best 'post fade' in other words after the sound of your guitar has faded away leaving the delay to create the atmospheric echo. A good quality delay also produces very little noise so doesn't need additional noise reduction. If you have a reverb pedal use it at the very last point before the amp.

If you have trouble

It's a pain but if you are using stomp boxes be prepared to invest in good quality short length guitar patch cables. All DC powered effects are more prone to noise than AC powered effects too. Batteries are particularly good at introducing noise and all sorts of errors into an otherwise perfectly good string of effects. If in doubt *change the battery first* before sending it back to the shop for repair. You'll be amazed at the difference a fresh battery can make.

If you have two or three battery powered effects you should also be thinking about a high quality mains DC adapter with enough outputs for all of your pedals.

7 ❖

Maintenance

Maintaining your guitar simply means you making sure that it keeps on sounding and playing the way you want it to. Maintenance is anything from wiping down your strings before you put it away, to a complete rebuild in a professional technician's shop. Basic maintenance is anything possible at home, safely on your kitchen tabletop without specialist tools or equipment.

Before we go any further I'd like to say that if you want to practice electronics or joinery, your instrument is probably the wrong place to start. Like that car advert when the car breaks down at a vital moment because the owner chose the wrong brand of spares, you don't want to risk messing up and possibly putting your instrument out of service until paying somebody else to fix the problem becomes possible. So it is vital to know what you are doing, and plan an escape route before you start.

Very often things go wrong not with the job you attempt but with another problem that appears usually just at the worst moment. Likewise If you haven't used a soldering iron before or if you aren't used to spray paints, then experiment on old materials first. You will get a better result and you will not have risked the appearance and resale value of your instrument. The good side is that with care and experience you'll find that many simple tasks don't take very long and can extend the life and desirability of your guitar.

Toolkit

Contact cleaner, Fast Fret, tape, cable ties, screws, batteries, files and rasps, 25 watt soldering iron, resin core solder, small Philips head screwdriver, small flat bladed screwdriver, small 'needle nose' pliers, standard pliers, small wire cutters, sharp bladed knife, jeweller's screwdriver set, small file, Allen keys, money, multimeter, mags, torch, stringwinder.

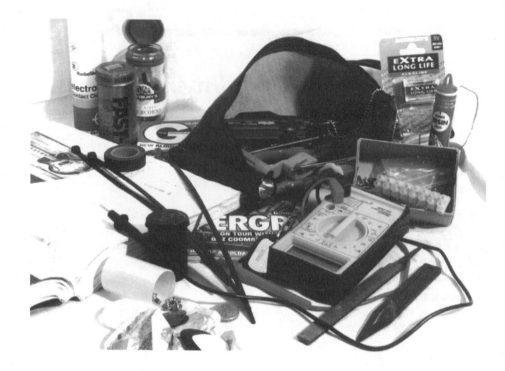

A collection of useful tools

Servicing

Everyday (if you play once a day)

* Wipe down the strings with a soft lint (dust) free cloth after each session.
* Wipe a light coating of Fast Fret over the strings to neutralise the acids in the moisture from your hands.

Every week (or after 12 -15 hours playing)

* All of the above plus
* Clean fingerboard with silicone polish then fit a new set of strings
* Check Intonation
* Check action
* Adjust machine head tension screws
* Check loose strap buttons

Once a month

* All of the above plus:
* Remove service plate or scratch plate
* Spray a little contact cleaner into each potentiometer
* Check for loose connections and dry solder joints

* Remove metal fragments from pickup pole pieces with 'Blu-Tack'
* With a cotton bud apply a very small amount of automotive silicone oil to intonation and action adjusting screws.
* Buff frets with synthetic steel wool and finish with light polish

Once a year

* All of the above plus:
* Check for neck distortion and adjust truss rod if necessary (see truss rod)
* Use synthetic steel wool to rub down the fingerboard, removing all traces of dirt.
* Use propriety guitar oil to finish the fingerboard
* Check frets for wear and replace if necessary

Setting up the electric guitar

Setting up means having your guitar brought right back up to specification, to be as good and hopefully better than it was when it left the factory. This means checking and adjusting each of these:

* Neck relief (truss rod adjustment)
* String height
* Pickup height
* Bridge adjustment
* Nut height
* Intonation
* Fingerboard condition
* Fret wear

Depending on the age and condition of the instrument a workshop set up will cost from around £30 upwards, not including new strings, and will take just a few days. But as always with a little care and the right tools most of these tasks can easily be approached by the player.

A word about guitar tuning and setup

Adjusting the action of the guitar is the first thing that many players do in the hope of either making their guitar easier to play, sound better or both. However a 'perfect' action isn't ever achieved simply by changing the height of the bridge or saddles. Tuning the action of your guitar is a little like tuning the strings. It's a combination of adjustments all acting together that keep your guitar playing just how you like it. Like a good mechanic the ability to recognise what a guitar needs only comes with experience, and just like a car the guitar needs a regular service to keep it tuned up.

Differences of 0.5 of a millimetre (1/64th of an inch) or even less can change a guitar's feel under your fingers. Because of this precision the action of your guitar can change overnight maybe in reaction to changes in humidity and air pressure. Putting a heavier set of strings on your guitar will certainly require action adjustment. This fine tuning can mean the difference between a guitar that's playable guitar and one that's not, yet some instruments go unadjusted for years.

Procedure for simple setup of a solid bodied electric guitar

Start with neck relief then adjust the nut before using the bridge to raise or lower string height and make any intonation adjustments. Whenever you adjust string height also check the intonation and vice versa. Many variables work together to make the guitar what it is.

Truss rod adjustment

The truss rod is used to adjust neck relief; the slight bow in the neck that must be there to accommodate the vibrating string at its widest point.

Important notice

Don't play or experiment with truss rod adjustment. I don't mean to be scary but ill considered or extreme adjustments can do permanent damage, possibly a new neck or at worst a new guitar! You can't make a poor neck into a good one or make your old guitar into a new one by simply hacking at the truss rod. But. If you are careful it's simple to make your guitar easier to play.

Your guitar wouldn't play if the neck was perfectly straight. Don't believe me? Check this out. Pick up your guitar and look closely at the low E string. Put the guitar in the playing position and pick the open E. You'll see the string vibrate as it describes a figure of eight many times a second. The vibration is widest at the centre of the string, above the twelfth fret. If the guitar neck was perfectly flat there would be no room for the string to vibrate. It needs a little bow (called relief) in the middle of the neck to allow room for this vibration to happen. The guitar neck naturally bows in the middle anyway. You'd imagine it would as there's nearly 200lbs of pressure trying to rip the neck clean off at the heel. Fortunately the guitar has a steel rod, anchored at one end of the neck to counterbalance this pulling by adding a little tension of its own.

Every string must be anchored at each end; the nut and the bridge. When a string is hit it will vibrate in an arc between these two points. If the string is open (unfretted) the note is called the fundamental – the lowest note that the string may produce. If the string is fretted the note will be higher but shorter.

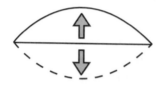

Truss rod adjustment is the first stage in setting up the guitar to play well. The purpose of truss rod adjustment is to set the neck relief for the vibrating string so it must be done with the guitar tuned to concert pitch.

To adjust the truss rod you'll need to get at the truss rod nut which is

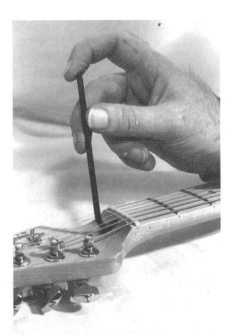

Using an Allen key to adjust
the truss rod

located either at the top of the guitar just above the nut or at the very end of the neck facing the rhythm pickup (sometimes obscured by the scratchplate). You might need to remove a small cover to get at the rod.

Depending on the make of your guitar the truss rod must be adjusted with a hexagonal Allen key, a nut spinner or a truss rod wrench, available from specialist guitar stores and suppliers. Before you adjust the rod measure the amount of neck relief by setting a capo at the first fret and stopping the string at the 12th fret with your finger. Use a set of automobile spark gap feelers to measure the distance between the top of the fifth fret and the bottom of the low E string. You'll find a tiny measurement between 0.2 and 0.4 mm, depending on your string gauge and make of guitar Any larger than this and it's either a bass guitar or in need of serious attention.

Essentially your aim is to optimise this distance to give maximum room for the string to vibrate, while making the guitar as easy as possible to play. If the gap between the bottom of the string and the top of the fret is too small then loosen the truss rod by one eighth of a turn. Retune and check the neck relief as before. If the gap is too large tighten the truss rod by an eighth and recheck. If you can't turn the nut, take the guitar to a repairer — never force or make large adjustments to the truss rod.

Bear in mind at all times that the guitar must be tuned to concert pitch when adjusting the truss rod and that truss rod adjustments must never be made to compensate for string height. The truss rod affects neck relief only.

So many people think that truss rod adjustment is the devil's work. However, these are also the sort of people who think that guitar playing starts with Hank and stops with Dave. Enough already. You are a thoughtful careful person aren't you? Just be careful out there.

Nut adjustment

Nut adjustment must be checked to ensure the correct height of the string above the first fret. Hold the guitar so it faces you and stop the low E string at the third fret. Now tap the string midway between the second and first. You should hear a click as the string meets the top of the first fret. This is a rule of thumb indicator as to the height of the nut. Ideally the low E string should just be free of the first fret with no more than a 0.5 mm gap between the fret and the string. If necessary use a fine round needle file to carefully deepen the slot.

Using a thin file to widen a nut slot

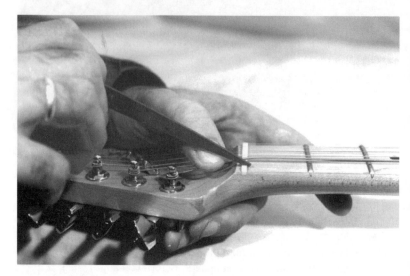

When filing or sawing a new slot always cut towards the fingerboard. Try and create a gently sloping cut with no rough sides. The width of the slot is vital as the string must be held in the slot without being able to move from side to side. If you cut too much material you'll have to fit a new nut.

Nut replacement

Use a fine scalpel to cut the finish around the nut and tap towards the headstock with a small hammer to break the glue bond. Replacement nuts are widely available, take the old nut to the store when choosing to make sure that you have the correct string spacing. Fit the new nut by removing any old glue and finish from the slot and applying PVA glue to the wood. Leave for at least 24 hours before working the new nut. Locking nuts and roller nuts need attention from specialist repairers.

Bridge adjustment

String height and intonation are set at the bridge. When adjusting string height make sure that the guitar is tuned to concert pitch. You will need one or more tools depending on the type of bridge that your guitar has.

A simple Tune-O-Matic bridge can be height adjusted with a slot screwdriver. The two bridge posts are large threaded bolts which are adjustable for height. Turn clockwise to lower string height and anti-clockwise to

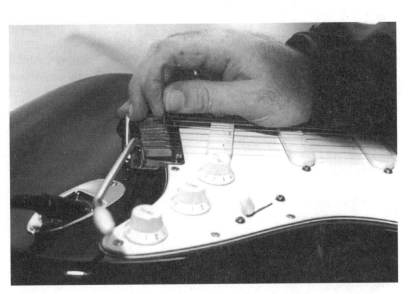

Adjusting string height on a
Fender bridge

raise string height. The Tune-O-Matic and Stop Bar types of bridge do not allow individual string height adjustment to compensate for neck radius.

To raise or lower the string height on a Fender bridge saddle, use a small Allen key to screw or unscrew small grub screws in each saddle. Raise each saddle slightly, check tuning and play along the neck. If the bridge piece is too low you'll experience string choke around the 13th fret. In this case the saddle must be raised slightly and action rechecked. Two grub screws are used for each saddle to allow compensation for the fingerboard radius but they must be adjusted in sympathy with neck relief and nut height for a perfect action. Check the intonation when bridge saddles are adjusted to the optimum height.

Adjust the bridge or saddles so that the high E string is around 1.5 – 2 mm above the 12th fret. The low E string should be around 2 – 3 mm above the 12th fret. These measurements will vary depending on your gauge of string and the way you like your guitar to play.

 INFO

Tremolo bridges are adjusted in the same way as Fender bridges, but particular attention must be paid to even out spring tension which will affect the height of the bridge.

String choke happens when the string height is too low and the strings are stopped by the frets

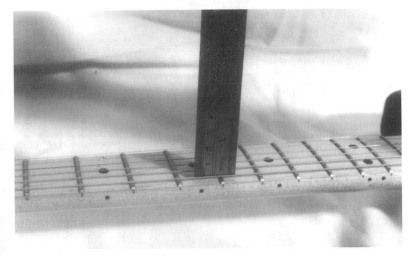

Measuring string height

You'd think that an old Fender would play like a dream wouldn't you? Well if you get to play one, be prepared for a shock. The first couple of years of Fender production produced guitars that were made with string height way above what we expect these days. Strats in 1954 had very narrow neck radius meaning that the high E string often had to be higher than usual at the nut to prevent the string slipping off the side of the neck.

Guitar string technology was pretty new in those days, and it wasn't until 1961 that Fender changed the specification of their pickups to match the new 'plain G' string sets that were becoming popular by slightly shortening the height of the 'G' pole piece to compensate for the louder string. Early Stratocasters were made to be used with high heavy pure nickel strings that suited the early pickups. All said and done , that 'vintage' sound is a combination of many things – not least the effort coming from the player!

Intonation

Intonation adjustments enable your guitar to play in tune. Intonation is the ability of a guitar to play in tune anywhere along the neck. This is dictated by fret spacing and string length. Fret spacing is set but string length will change depending on the make and weight of your guitar strings. Fractional changes in the weight of your strings will mean that the intonation will need adjusting. Tremolo bridges must also be regularly checked.

Using a screwdriver to adjust intonation

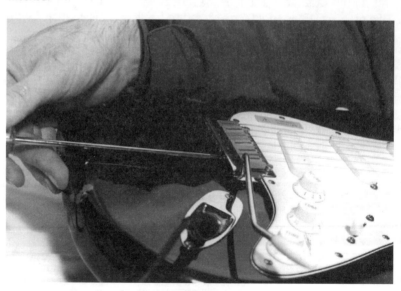

1 Use a guitar tuner to tune the low E string
2 Stop the string at the 12th fret and measure the pitch again. Both fretted and open string should be exactly in tune.
3 If the tuner shows that the fretted note is flat use a screwdriver or key to move the bridge or bridge piece forward towards the pickups. If the string is sharp move the bridge piece back.
4 Repeat the process until both fretted and open strings are in tune.
5 Repeat for each string.

If you change bridge height then the intonation must be adjusted again.

String spacing

This is a characteristic of your guitar but like the scale length is another one that's fixed. The string spacing is the distance between each string measured between the low E and A strings at the nut and bridge.

Standard string spacing for various types of guitar

Spacing in mm	At nut	At bridge
Acoustic guitar	10.5	6.5
Electric Guitar (stop bar)	9	6
Les Paul	10.5	6.5
Telecaster	11.5	6
Stratocaster	10.2	6.5

A Floyd Rose tremolo bridge on a Fender guitar has a wider spacing than normal. Replacement pickups for this kind of bridge are called 'F' (Fender) spaced.

These four steps will keep your guitar in tune and always good to play. Later repairs such as fret wear and pickup replacement can be tackled during your guitar's annual visit to the doctor but unless you pay regular attention to these first four steps, it'll never be as good as it could be.

Other maintenance

Pickup maintenance

To make an old pickup sound better try a little maintenance. Remove the pickup covers from humbucking pickups if you like a neat utility look, but beware that this might increase the risk of interference, especially with humbucking pickups. If the copper windings are visible, protect the exposed coils with tape. Be very careful – if you break the coil the pickup won't work and will be very expensive or even impossible to repair.

Over time, small particles of metal may become attracted to the magnetic pole pieces. Too many of these particles interfere with the lines of force

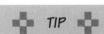

TIP

It's OK to experiment with pickup height as no lasting damage is possible to either guitar or amplifier simply by adjusting the height of each pickup. However you might want to make a note of the distance between the strings and the pickups before you experiment.

A sticky pad will remove dirt
and rust from a pickup

and can affect your sound. Remove dirt and small particles from each pole piece and the windings by pressing gently with a small 'sticky pad' or 'Blu Tack'

Pickup height

To maximise the effectiveness of your existing pickups they must be adjusted to sit at just the right point under the string. If the pickups are too close the magnetic pull will cause poor intonation.

If the pickups are too far away the string will lose volume. A pickup that is set very close to the strings will affect string vibration, cause over-tones and even dead notes. Fender Stratocasters often suffer from this problem especially if players mistakenly raise the height of each of the three pickups to almost meet the strings while searching for more output. This has the effect of over-magnetising the wound strings and leads to a very peculiar sound.

Adjust pickups to sit at just
the right point under the
string. If the pickups are too
close the magnetic pull will
cause poor intonation.

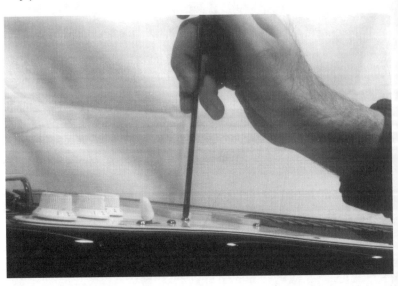

The pickups should be lowered slightly at the bass end to remove this effect, lowering the pickup at the treble end doesn't make so much difference owing to the thinner treble strings.

Pole piece adjustment is crucial. Good pole piece adjustment is between 1 and 3 mm above the pickup cover. If the pole piece is below the cover it won't work well at all. Some 'vintage' single coil pickups have non adjustable staggered pole pieces which are pre-set at the right height for each string. Overall pickup height is adjustable by the height adjustment screws which are usually at the side of each pickup.

Frets

Frets can get worn out, but having them replaced isn't expensive. Look after your frets by keeping a piece of OOO grade steel wool to rub over the frets every time you change strings. This will keep down the corrosion caused by the moisture in your fingers and will make your guitar even easier to play. I've found a synthetic wool pad at DIY stores which is water washable and finer for a better finish. Polish the fret with the wire wool and buff with a soft cloth. When you've finished polishing the frets rub a little fingerboard oil directly into the fingerboard to disguise marks and add lustre.

Some (ahem) teachers recommend that you soak your fingertips in surgical spirit to harden them up. I used to do the same thing with conkers when I was eight. Didn't work then, doesn't work now. I wouldn't recommend that you bake your fingers in an oven either. If holding down a string hurts your fingers it means that the action is too high. Have it reset. Remember that a little gentle pressure is all that's required to stop the string, you don't need to press hard at all. Just press down behind the fret. Holding down a string will feel uncomfortable for maybe a week after you start playing, after that you'll be having too much fun to worry about it.

Minor scratches and cleaning

Many minor and unimportant scratches will become visible if you hold the guitar to the light. These are usually invisible to the observer and do very little to devalue your guitar, in fact some of these scratches may have been caused during the manufacture of the guitar. However every guitar will suffer more obvious unsightly scratches which aren't difficult to remove.

Many guitars, especially those from the Far East, will have polyester finishes which were applied in the factory by 'dipping' the guitar. This process enables the manufacturer to quickly produce an attractive finish. This finish is very brittle and as it is plastic based is easily marked by heat. For this reason I wouldn't recommend the use of 'DIY' power tools when repairing small areas of damage.

Light scratches

If your guitar is scratched, remove the strings and mask the area around the scratch with 'low tack' tape and newspaper paper. Leave 5 mm around the scratch for your finishing to blend with the existing finish. Take a cloth and dab T Cut onto the scratched area. Rub firmly in a circular motion and periodically add more T Cut. After a short while the scratch will begin to disappear as the abrasive T Cut removes finish around the scratch.

When the scratch is nearly invisible wipe the area with the second cloth and repeat the procedure with Brasso until the scratch has disappeared. Finally repeat with Windolene to remove scratches caused by the T Cut and Brasso. Eventually the scratch will be 'polished out'. It's important not to be tempted to use power tools for this as it's extremely difficult to prevent the tool cutting into the scratched area. What you don't need is to be adding finish to an area which was undamaged!

Tools
Two soft cotton dusters, 'T-Cut', 'Brasso', ' Windolene', tape, soft paper.

Cleaning the guitar
Prolonged use of household polishes with a heavy silicone content can cause the tone of your acoustic guitar to become muffled and attract dust and dirt through static electricity charge. The biggest enemy that your guitar faces is you, the player. Use a proprietary guitar polish to clean off the grease and muck that your fingers inevitably transfer to your guitar. When cleaning use one soft cloth to polish, another to buff. Keep a light paintbrush handy for getting into the cracks and spaces in pickups and bridges and lay the buffing cloth along the fingerboard when storing the guitar in it's case.

Take a tip from violin players and use a dab of olive oil on the fingerboard from time to time. It prevents drying out and brings the wood up very well. Extra Virgin is preferred over blended (grin).

Oiling the fingerboard prevents drying out and brings the wood up very well

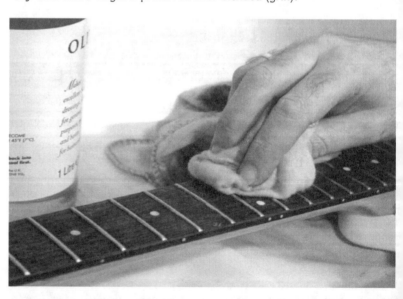

Frets can be cleaned with metal polish if necessary but always mask the fingerboard with tape. Brasso and other abrasive polishes can not be

removed from wood grain and will dry a contrasting colour to the dark wood which looks terrible. Use masking tape on each side of the fret and use wadding polish such as 'Dura-glit' which doesn't contain the abrasive. Pro refinishers use jeweller's polish and tiny finishing wheels.

Customising and refinishing

If you have an old or damaged guitar lying around, why not give it some new life with a new finish?. Even if the guitar doesn't play or sound just as you'd like at least you'll have something eye catching for stage, and no-one else will ever have another guitar like yours.. a real custom job without the expense!

Refinishing an old guitar is a good idea if you want to get the most from an instrument that would otherwise just be gathering dust, and if it's in poor condition before you start then you aren't losing anything by making it your own.

Caution! It's a bad idea (a *very* bad idea) to refinish a guitar with a resale value of more than £150. In other words if you could sell your guitar tomorrow (before refinishing it) for more than £150 then don't refinish! Why? Unless you are a famous artist already it's unlikely that your artwork will suit the next guy down the road. Remember that guitar players are becoming increasingly conservative and for many people a guitar made in 1958 is much more attractive than one made in 1998.

In resale terms, a guitar will fetch more if it is in the same condition that it was when it left the factory. Customers generally don't like to be reminded that the guitar has been messed with, especially when you consider that a proper refinishing job requires the complete stripping down and removal of all parts. Moreover, don't even consider part exchanging a refinished guitar for a brand new one, you'll be laughed out of the shop.

No, refinishing your guitar is the equivalent of nailing your colours to the mast. If you like the guitar already, if it plays just right for you, if you are *certain* that you'll never part with it and if you bought it for next to nothing then go right ahead. Remember this – to the guy in the shop – original is best.

OK let's begin

A basic refinishing job doesn't require a lot of tools, doesn't really require much specialist knowledge and can be successfully done with the help of your high street auto store and DIY shop. To do this right you'll need to take a couple of weeks off playing or borrow another guitar to play while you refinish your own. It all takes time but is worth it in the end. If you aren't the patient type then it's probably best not start this, the biggest mistake you can make (and the easiest way to mess it up) is to rush this job. You will need:

* An old guitar
* Power tools for stripping old finish
* Working space (it's a messy job)
* Wood filler
* Basic toolkit (see previous chapter)
* Sanding equipment
* Spray booth or spray area

Stripping down

Preparation is important for a good result, time invested at this point will produce a better finish and a much quicker job!

Carefully!! Remove knobs, buttons and external fittings. Have a small stock of plastic bags handy and store each fitting in its own bag together with the fixings. Label the bags and store carefully. Stratocaster and Telecaster guitars, or any model with pickups attached to a scratchplate which extends under the strings, are easy to dissemble. After removing the strings and scratchplate screws, carefully lift the plate from the front of the guitar.

Care must be taken as a short piece of wire connects the bridge to the rear of the master volume control. Another short piece of screened cable connects the pickup assembly to the jack plug. Make a note of where these cables connect (mark connections with yellow chinagraph pencil if necessary) and remove both cables with a low wattage soldering iron.

Finally remove the bridge, teardrop plate and any other surface hardware until the body is completely free of fittings. Les Paul guitars are more difficult as the control pots, switch and pickups are mounted in separate cavities in the guitar. Access is from the rear so place enough foam or other protective material on your work surface to cover the neck and headstock.

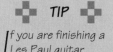

Control knobs should just pull off with a little pressure. If you have difficulty check for grub screws in the side of each knob. Never apply extreme force. Unscrew nuts and shakeproof washer from each shaft. Remove all service plates and examine wiring. It is impossible to refinish a Les Paul guitar without removing the pickups which have to be completely disconnected from the electronics cavity. Tag each wire with a small self adhesive sticker such as the kind found in stationers for identifying files. Now make a wiring diagram noting the colour and connections of each wire. If you have access to a Polaroid camera take a picture. In short you need to know exactly how to wire the guitar back together again in a weeks time.

The Les Paul pickup selector switch is located on the upper bout of the guitar and the wiring is reached by removing a small plate from the rear. The cable connecting the pickup selector can be disconnected with a soldering iron and the pickup selector can then be unscrewed and removed.

Leave the cable inside the guitar as you'll save a lot of hassle when you come to assemble the guitar again. Les Paul guitars have four threaded studs set into the surface of the guitar, two for the stop tailpiece and two for the Tune-O-Matic bridge. These are usually difficult to remove and need carefully capping with artist's masking tape before refinishing.

The neck

If the subject is a Stratocaster, carefully remove the neck plate and draw the screws from the neck. You may find the neck has been 'shimmed' ,in which case some material might fall from the neck joint. Carefully pick this up and store. Any guitar with a bolt on neck is a much better subject for refinishing than a set neck guitar because the neck and headstock are simple maple, requiring nothing more than a coat of clear varnish. Most cosmetic refinishing jobs leave these parts alone, perhaps with just a new colour for the headstock face.

Removing the original finish

Bear in mind that the finish on many guitars is actually designed to improve or enhance the sound of the guitar. You will find that the character of your sound will have completely changed after refinishing and it is difficult to tell in advance if this is going to be a good or bad thing. On the other hand you won't be losing anything if it's an old guitar and an eye catching finish will add to your live show, even if you just use the guitar for one or two songs.

The original finish must be removed even if you are painting the guitar with a solid colour. The right method of removing finish very much depends on the guitar you are working on. Budget Japanese, Korean and Indonesian guitars are often finished in polyester which will only come off with a heavy duty belt sander. If you are good with power tools carefully remove the existing finish down to the wood. Rotating disc sanders can't be controlled and can easily cut the wood leaving marks which have to be painfully sanded out. Palm or hand sanders are better but don't have the weight to cut through 3 mm of finish. Use a professional belt sander available from any hire shop. It is really important that you don't cut into the wood with the power tool as any cuts or dents will have to be filled then sanded again, so take your time.

If you really can't face stripping the polyester from your guitar then why not simply spray paint over the polyester after lightly sanding the guitar to provide a key for the aerosol primer.

Guitars finished in cellulose lacquer can be stripped of their finish using a DIY paint stripper such as Nitromors. If you plan to use this method I'd strongly recommend testing it on a small area first. As you have the guitar stripped back, test the stripper in one of the pickup or control cavities. Leave for a period of time according to manufacturer's instructions then scrape off the loose paint with a filling knife before wiping the guitar down with a clean wet cloth to remove any excess stripper.

This approach takes more time but will produce a better result as the stripper is able to enter all the cavities that sanding just won't reach. It's

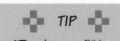

TIP

*D*on't use a DIY heat gun. Guitar finish and gloss paint react to extreme heat in completely different ways, you may lose the guitar, your eyebrows, your house, etc. Just don't!

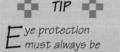

TIP

*E*ye protection must always be worn when working with power sanding equipment.

also marginally less messy and doesn't produce a lot of dust, which is important especially if you are planning to paint the guitar in the same working space. However, you will need to take care removing the paint stripper. Caution at this point. Always wear gloves and eye protection when using paint stripper. If your guitar has plastic inlays or bindings set into the wood the chemical stripper may melt these and damage them.

Smoothing the wood

The wood used to make the guitar has a big influence on the way you might refinish it. For instance laminated guitars obviously look terrible with a clear finish. Therefore, if it's anything other than real wood you'll be looking at refinishing it in solid colour.

Start with medium/coarse sandpaper and work along the grain around the whole body. Then use a medium paper and repeat, finally down to fine grade paper. The aim is to remove any legacy dents or nicks while rubbing away any damage caused by removing the finish. When the guitar is shaped and smooth, clean the wood along the grain with a soft cloth dipped in white spirit to remove dust and grease. Then leave to dry overnight. If you are going to paint the guitar you'll need to fill any small holes with filler and sand smooth

Refinishing

Hint! Art books are full of groovy artworks with loads of good ideas, and custom car books are even better. Tattoo books and Spray Can art books are usually good places to look for 'off the wall' ideas. In fact spray can artists are very useful to know as a good one will know how to create a big impact in a small space! Just don't try your ideas on any walls that you don't own already!

Pretty much the only practical way to apply a professional high gloss finish at home is to use automotive aerosol paint. And the best range of colours is down at your local car spares store. Don't skimp on primer, if you don't prime it the colour will just slide off the wood.

By far the most difficult thing to do is find a good working space. Spray paint goes everywhere, bedrooms and kitchens are not a good idea. If you don't have a garage then use the great outdoors on a dry day without wind. Wherever you use spray paint you must wear a dust mask. The key to the whole process is patience. You'll need 10 or 15 coats to get a good finish. A high gloss coat comparable to a factory finish is within your reach with a little care. The secret is to wait at least 6 hours between coats and rub down with very fine (400 grade) wet and dry paper after each coat. DIY stores sell sponge blocks covered in wet and dry abrasive.

Remember that any nicks in the wood are really going to show up under a spray finish so the key is preparation. If you are doing this at home the best approach is to do it over a week adding a coat in the morning and one in the evening leaving it to dry while you sleep or go to school or work. Don't forget that colours combine to produce different results. I got a great candy apple red colour from an orange base coat with a primary red top coat.

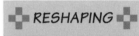

HINT

*L*es Paul guitars usually have these bindings (and a non-removable neck, and more wiring).

RESHAPING

*W*hy not customise the shape of your guitar? There is a lot of scope for removing wood completely or reshaping the top. Cut holes in it, add carvings or reshape the whole thing. How about rethinking the way the strap buttons are attached to the guitar?

Final fixing

This is where the fun begins. You have a new instrument with limitless possibilities. How about painting it black then going to the scrap yard and picking badges of old motors, polishing them up and screwing them to the top?

Alternatively, going to the DIY store and choosing stencils in pastel colours. How about obtaining some gold leaf and gold plating your guitar? (it's cheaper than you think). On the other hand, smash an old mirror into small pieces and make a mosaic mirror guitar! Cover it in fur! It sounds naff but a good place to go for ideas is to buy an interior decorating magazine.

Whatever you do, remember that finish and materials affect the sound of your instrument. In general a heavyweight guitar will sound darker, a light guitar will have more treble. If you take wood away from the guitar you will alter the tone forever. A very experienced luthier (guitar maker) can use this to create a guitar that is tuned to perfection, but for inexperienced people this is very difficult. As a rule of thumb it's best not to vary wildly from the original shape of the guitar and not to cut too many holes in it, especially don't cut any holes behind the bridge or near any strap buttons.

The Iron Cross

I caught an old and very abused Yamaha RGX that someone was throwing out. The guitar looked like it had been stored without a case in a very damp place, maybe in a wardrobe or stair cupboard. The strings had been left on the guitar, so even after a long period of poor storage the tension had maintained neck alignment and could still be adjusted. The pickups and frets were badly corroded, as were the electronics, but the chrome plated Floyd Rose style bridge and steel tuners were OK. The Yamaha has

Unfinished Yamaha RGX

seen some heavy use as the frets and bridge were worn and corroded, but the most important parts (the parts that couldn't be made at home or replaced cheaply) were still serviceable.

The condition and colour of the guitar indicated that the best thing to do would be to apply another finish on top of the existing one . Stripping and sanding wouldn't be necessary as the finish was in relatively good condition with just a few nicks and dents. I had already refinished an old fireplace in artist's 'crackle glaze' which gives a terrific 'cracked porcelain' finish, and I was itching to see how the effect would work on a guitar. The Yamaha had the right off white base coat and seemed to be a perfect candidate for refinishing. The object was to produce an 'aged' effect without too much sparkle or gloss, I even wanted the guitar to look a little rough and ready, like it had a couple of centuries worth of use.

Step 1 Stripping and saving

The first thing to do was strip the guitar down, removing the neck and every piece of hardware, until all that was left was the bare body. The strings, electronics and badly rusted pickups were all thrown away but I saved the pickup and mounting ring screws which are expensive to buy. I also liked the aged look of the screw heads which fitted in with the tatty and battered look I had in mind for the guitar.

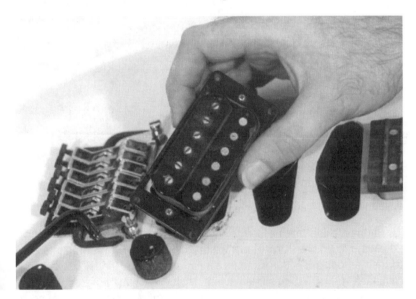

Removing pickups and bridge from the guitar

Step 2 Cleaning and shaping

The neck needed the most work as the fingerboard and frets were in a very poor condition. The first thing that needed to be done was to remove the muck that was corroding the frets and destroying the rosewood fingerboard. I used a piece of synthetic steel wool to remove the worst of the damage, and finished off with a toothbrush around the side of the frets. The fingerboard was badly pitted and care had to be taken to remove every scrap of residue. On removing the green mess I discovered

Using synthetic steel wool to clean frets and fingerboard

that the frets were badly worn and in need of a good fretmill. A complete re-fret would have been preferable but to save time the frets were just smoothed and crowned in a few hours. After the frets and fingerboard had been rescued I applied fingerboard dressing then olive oil for sheen and condition. Thankfully the nut was in good condition.

A jigsaw adds some drama to the Yamaha headstock

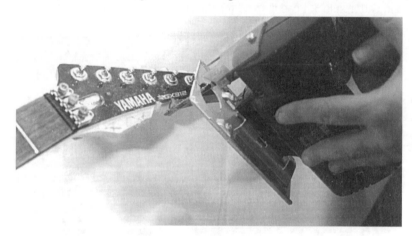

The next thing that needed to be done was to re-shape the headstock. I'd always loved the 'Kitty Hawk' paint jobs that World War II pilots gave to their aeroplanes and I wanted a similar appearance. The RGX headstock reminded me of a bird's beak which I chopped with a jigsaw to make teeth and lips. Later I will add some eyes and more detail. The body needed less attention as the polyester had stopped the damp getting to the wood itself. All that was necessary was a good clean, first with white spirit to remove all the years of dried gunk and then with a little silicone based polish.

When the body was clean and dry I applied stickers that I had found in a old model aircraft shop. The Germanic look is an accident as these were the best of a limited stock but they add a great deal to the finished guitar.

Applying self-adhesive
stickers to the body

Step 3 A new finish

Crackle glaze is a fine art product invented to give artwork an aged effect. It's a water based glaze which is brushed over a semi-dry oil based varnish and then heated with a hairdryer to crack the surface. Oil paint is then rubbed into the very fine cracks and the glaze is sealed with oil based varnish. This effect is very dramatic and it's difficult to believe that the Burnt Umber oil paint isn't the result of hundreds of years of grime and fire damage. It's not a finish designed with the guitar in mind so five coats of polyurethane varnish were used to seal the cracked glaze to protect it from many hours of plectrum and gig damage. The oil finish was left to dry for three days before the first sealing coat was applied and care had to be taken when brushing the sealing coats on to avoid drips.

The difficult part was handling the guitar while the very fragile oil paint was drying. Before I started work I manufactured a 'handle' which was screwed to the guitar in place of the neck, and this was used whenever the guitar had to be held and could be trapped safely in the vice while the guitar was drying. The headstock was treated to a rough coat of red and white paint for 'teeth' and 'lips'.

Step 4 Fittings and fixtures

I'd bought a new Korean made Kent Armstrong pickup with this guitar in mind, but the pickup came without mounting screws and the base plate wouldn't accept the Japanese ones that had been rescued from the Yamaha. Eventually I decided to splash out on a new pickup for my Les Paul (Seymour Duncan '59 – ace!) and used the F (Floyd Rose) spaced DiMarzio Air Classic that was on the Les Paul for the new guitar. The DiMarzio Air Classic now suits the Yamaha's Floyd Rose bridge just right and the Les Paul got a whole new sound from the new Seymour Duncan pickup at the same time! The new guitar was bound to be a no frills rock guitar so both single coil slots were left unfilled and the electronics stripped right back to one new volume control and a new jack socket. The volume control is also a push pull switch for coil split. Later I'll add a series/parallel switch where the tone control would be.

By this time the 'aged' look of the new guitar was dictating the direction of the fittings and an old 1970's Mighty Mite solid brass knob was found in the bottom of a drawer. Suitably corroded it suited the damaged look perfectly.

Removing dirt with an old toothbrush and spray lubricant

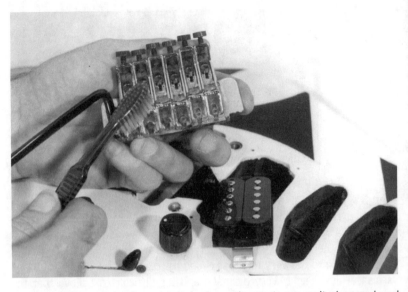

The bridge was badly corroded where the parts weren't chromed and so needed stripping down, cleaning and oiling in all places. This is a really tedious job but needed to be done, the result was that a poorly performing bridge was made to work much better. WD 40 was used to smooth the action of the bridge pieces and fine tuners.

Step 5 Setting up and pickup

By far the most difficult job was resetting and adjusting the Yamaha floating tremolo. Years of poor maintenance had taken the tension from the springs to the point where the tremolo claw had to be wound right back to apply enough tension. As the bridge had been stripped down, the action and intonation had to be set and reset for each string as the spring tension went up and down. In the end I made a wooden wedge which I cut to the right dimensions to hold the bridge solid at about the height that a set of well adjusted springs would do. This enabled me to adjust action and intonation while the bridge remained firm. Then I slackened the strings off, removed the wedge and replaced the springs, tuned the guitar and adjusted the springs to hold the bridge level at the same point as the wedge. The guitar needed a shim under the bolt on neck but eventually the string height and intonation were set. Neck relief needed some adjustment but came right in the end.

The only problems remaining with it are a dead spot on the 13th fret where the fretmill didn't come right and a worn second fret. Apart from that – it's OK.

The DiMarzio pickup proved a little more of a problem. The replacement Seymour Duncan was supplied without a mounting ring so I had to leave the DiMarzio ring on the Les Paul. The Yamaha pickup that was originally fitted to the RGX was very tall, leaving the mounting ring very shallow, too shallow for the Dimarzio pickup. The result is that even after winding the DiMarzio right up to the top it's still 10mm away from the

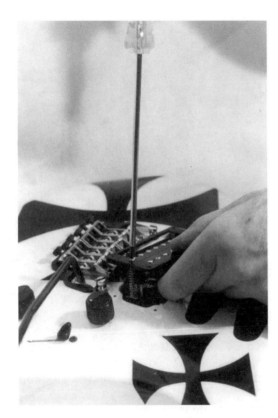

strings. A new mounting ring must be bought. Its not expensive but hey guys – I mean I paid loads for that pickup, couldn't you have put a mounting ring in the box! The only other problem was the cable purchased for the connection between the jack socket and the volume pot. I ordered budget screened cable which gave the worst sound I ever heard – a replacement length of oxygen free cable proved much better. The moral – spend as much as is practical on the parts that matter!

The result

The 'Iron Cross' retains some of its original Yamaha manner. The RGX was a typical eighties guitar with lightweight body and a fussy tremolo system – both of which my new guitar has inherited. However the addition of a proper pickup and the stripping away of the cost effective Yamaha electronics has brought out a much simpler beast with a louder voice.

In humbucking mode the DiMarzio is very full and dirty but anxious for every squeal and scrape – pinched harmonics especially. With the coil split engaged the DiMarzio turns into a single coil with a single coil sound, surprisingly not much of a drop in volume but a noticeable loss of lower midrange sounds although the bass end is still there.

Action is higher than I'd like – no matter how much I tweaked it I couldn't compensate for the too simple 'twin bolt' arrangement of the bridge height adjusters. The tremolo arm is too close to the body, I'd like

The finished body with crackle glaze, burnt umber paint and stickers

much more travel but as soon as it starts sounding dramatic the arm hits the deck!

Overall I like it. The aged look is very effective and with a set of 'Skinny Top and Heavy Bottom' strings it sounds like a piano in a lift shaft! Just what I wanted it to do. I'll use it in my band for two or three of the more dramatic numbers, whatever happens it'll always have my name on it.

If I had to do it all again...

* I'd re-fret it rather than wishing it to be finished.
* I'd compare the height of the old Yamaha pickup with the new one and make sure I had a new mounting ring.
* I'd be more adventurous with the electronics – active maybe?
* I'd plug and fill the bridge posts and fit a brand new bridge.

The cost of refinishing and upgrading an old guitar

Yamaha RGX310	0:00
DiMarzio Air Classic	50:00
Electronic parts	15:00
Fittings	5:00
Glaze	2:50
Varnish	2:99
Stickers	2:50
Total	£87:99

Because it was rescued, the Yamaha didn't cost. The electronic components were purchased from a specialist supplier in Bristol and may be available cheaper from your local electronics store. Windsor and Newton crackle glaze is available from any fine arts supplier. Ronseal varnish and brushes available from any DIY superstore. I used a satin finish but high gloss is available. Stickers available from certain specialist model shops or model fair if one is near you. Knobs and screws from the bottom of my toolkit.

'Iron Cross' custom electric guitar £87.99

Buying and selling guitars

Most people have an idea of what guitar they want long before they walk into the store. This idea comes from doing what you are doing now; reading books, magazines, watching TV, listening to music etc. A lot of people buy a guitar because a particular player either plays one or (this is the important part) 'says' they play one. My advice is to wait until you get to see the person in concert and then look at the instruments on stage. Plenty of guitars get left in the truck, even the ones that appear in those good looking adverts. It's not uncommon for an artist to publicly endorse a guitar or amp that is only ever used backstage for warming up!

Eventually we build up a picture of a guitar that will do what we want and then we go around finding the guitar (or one similar) at the right price. So we have an idea, but how do we *know* which guitar is right when two or three fall into the frame? Here is my patented, never wrong method of getting the right guitar at the right price. Ready?

How much?

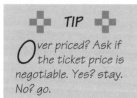

TIP

Over priced? Ask if the ticket price is negotiable. Yes? stay. No? go.

Keep an eye on prices in other stores and magazines so you'll know if a guitar is over (or under) priced.

Brand new

If the guitar is brand new, ask yourself 'when was this guitar sent to the dealer' (don't ask the guy in the shop). Just recently? Price probably not negotiable but gets marks for fashion and resale and good chance of store discount. Last six months? One unpopular guitar or did the store buy loads and are bringing them out slowly at current (varying) prices? Last year? It's probably a lemon which has been shipped around from shop to shop trying to find a buyer. Watch out for these, they usually have brand new strings and a big ticket at the front of the rack. More than two years? It's second hand...

Look carefully at 'the price point', that's industry talk for how much a guitar can retail for. Every major manufacturer makes to a particular price, and you need to stick at this point when comparing guitars. Bear in mind that below £350 the manufacturer either saves on fittings or finish. It's usually the fittings that suffer because the finish will sell the guitar. Decide whether purple sunburst or above average pickups are better for you. Above £350 the finish evens out as fittings and tonewood start to grab more of the maker's costs.

Judge each model on its own merits, even identical models from the same maker. Brand new guitars can vary wildly from instrument to instrument and often present more problems than second hand models. It is crucial how the distributor checks the guitar before it is delivered to the shop. Often budget guitars are 'batch tested' on arrival at the warehouse which means that only one in every delivery from the maker will be unpacked and checked over. In some shops with a high turnover this could mean that apart from a quick tune up, a guitar may not have been looked over since leaving the factory, so check for missing screws, loose frets, etc. Also ask the salesperson if a setup is included in the price.

Guitars over £500 are usually checked and set up before they leave the factory and by the distributor when they arrive in the UK. The distributor will then give the guitar a comprehensive setup leaving only final adjustments to the eventual owner. If the purchase price does not include a setup and the guitar hasn't been set up at the factory then you'll need to add £20 plus a couple of days without the guitar before it'll be perfect.

Guitars that haven't been set up will play out of tune and won't give the satisfaction you expect for your money. Although dealers and distributors try and check the guitars that pass through their hands, very often the sheer volume and economics of the guitar industry make anything more than a simple look over impossible. For this reason you should expect to do a little work on any guitar under £300 when you get it home, or pay for a setup at the shop if you aren't confident. If a guitar doesn't feel exactly right but appears to be a good price and brand new check with the shop to see if anything can be done before you buy it. Whatever you do, it is certainly a good idea to try two or three examples of the same model as guitars vary from piece to piece.

Second hand

Look at the condition of the guitar. Mint (factory new) used guitars are a bad bet. A tatty second hand with the right sort of wear has already had the problems ironed out and played well enough for the previous owner to get some good use out of it before moving on. Look for:

* Scratched pickup covers.
* Less chrome on jack sockets, bridge and screw heads.
* Smooth frets with a little wear.

But did the previous user move on because the cost of bringing it back up to spec outweighed the cost of a new instrument? In which case look out for:

* Worn frets with shallow areas under the G, B and E strings before the first fret.
* Loose and slipping machine heads.

* Excess wear to bridge parts, especially missing intonation and height adjustment screws.
* Evidence of damaged or excess wear to truss rod cover/scratchplate screws.
* Damage to the headstock caused by dropping (especially on Les Paul guitars).
* Hardware (especially pickups) which weren't part of the instruments original spec.
* Cracks around the heel and low strap button (indications of the guitar dropping from a broken strap) or poorly finished repairs.

What's the 'best price?'

* To you: It's how much you have to spend less any discount through negotiation.
* To the store: It's how much they paid, less incentives (freebie strings etc.) plus usual mark-up.
* To the market: It's the guitar's future collectible value.

So getting the best price is the art of balancing all these three prices and coming out with a deal that suits everyone. From a buyer's point of view it's vital that you put yourself in a strong position before you start to negotiate. That means having the wherewithal (the money, moolah, cash, spondoolicks etc.) available on the day. No promises, projections or assumptions please... And if you have a guitar to sell that means making a decision for yourself..

Part exchange or private sale?

A collectible guitar with a real resale value will be more attractive to a store than a mass produced instrument of a few years old. However, neither will achieve maximum potential in a trade. The store will try to resell your guitar for the trade in price plus a mark-up, and they will still have to try and be competitive. And who wants to shop at a store filled with undesirable second or third hand guitars? A good rule of thumb: if you 'couldn't sell your guitar for more than £200 privately, don't expect a good deal at trade in, and if your guitar would realistically make more than £200 then here are a few tips for maximising your trade-in value:

* Do not customise, box fresh is best.
* Change strings, check intonation and action and go through the six month service plan outlined earlier. Even spend some money on a setup.
* Find a case to trade in with it, it makes the guitar easier to sell.
* Take your original receipt (and some ID if they don't know you).

The only time you might have an advantage with a trade in is if you happen to own an instrument which has a value to a collector but which isn't widely known. A store can sell this kind of instrument to another collector at a higher price than you would get from the local paper, unless you were prepared to advertise in a trade paper.

Looking for the guitar

Where to look? Go to the magazine stand and buy a few titles. Guitar mags live on advertising and the best carry large two page spreads with prices and details. Now that home PC's are widespread there's even been a move towards 'advertorial', with stores including short 100 word reviews of gear that they particularly like, or just want to sell quickly. If this was a book on synth/sampler/SSHO equipment I'd say – 'give 'em a call – find the right price and slap out your credit card'. Why? Because the best home computer equipment is the stuff that comes direct from the factory. Untouched by human hand until you get your mitts on it. The last thing you want is the Saturday afternoon shop assistant taking it home for the weekend to sample the best bits off it before sending on to you.

Tanglewood Super Six

Guitars are a different thing altogether. A good guitar store will have unpacked, closely inspected and even played most of the instruments in stock before you get it. In addition, remember that guitars vary wildly from instrument to instrument. The only rule without exception is that buying guitars by mail order is a very bad idea. The best thing to do is to set aside a whole Saturday and after making a few exploratory telephone calls, go and take a look. Be prepared to come back with nothing if what they have isn't good enough, or isn't what you want.

Buying and selling guitars

A good guitar store will show you how the switches work, where to plug it in and what to do if it goes wrong. Remember that you have a year's warranty on any shop item unless you've agreed otherwise in writing. That means accepting a receipt with 'sold as seen' or 'trade sale' written down. In this case don't pay until you have a better understanding with the store. Any guitar shop that intends to stay in business will fix small faults as they occur, maybe even taking it back for a few days to put something right. Don't stretch the point by turning up eight weeks later asking for new strings though.

Some people buy guitars just to sell them on at a profit. This can be a good thing or a bad thing. A guitar is meant to give pleasure, so what's the point of leaving it on top of your wardrobe – especially when it could be earning you some money? In addition, this kind of trading in guitars drives up prices. How can a fifty year old guitar be worth £40,000?. Your average player isn't making that much money. The people who have £40,000 to spend on a guitar are more likely to be collectors who might store the guitar for a few years and then sell it back at a much higher price. So the guitar doesn't get played again and is even more unlikely to be back in the public domain when it comes up in auction. On the other hand it is the collector who will maintain the instrument in its original

Guitar collection backstage
including Strats, Jaguars –
and furry straps!

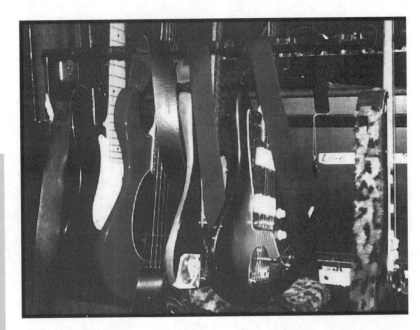

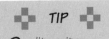

condition as if it were a museum piece, sometimes spending many thousands on restoration. It is a much bigger argument than I can go into in this book with opinions on either side.

Buying at auction

There's no rule that says anyone can't bid at auction and if you are planning to buy at auction here are a few things to bear in mind.

Finding a bargain at an auction is about as likely as Paul McCartney getting a job at my local McDonalds. Auctions artificially raise prices because they attract specialists to the saleroom and then get them to compete for one or two good lots. Anyone can bid but only if they have registered their intention on arriving. When you do this you are given a paddle with a number on it and you bid by raising the paddle. Don't worry about 'Nods and winks', if the auctioneer doesn't know you personally you'll need to formally bid. Once auctioneer has registered your bid by noting the number on your paddle there's no going back so be very sure that you know what you are doing.

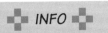

Instruments are sold as 'lots'. Lots are viewed before the auction, but playing or trying is normally out of the question without an appointment. Each lot has a reserve price which the bidding will start at. The auctioneer's job is to raise that price – the referee act is just for show. You may find that the reserve (starting) price is just under what you'd pay in a shop and if the auctioneer doesn't get the price that he is looking for – he'll take it out of auction. So have a price in mind and don't get dragged in.

FAKER MAKER

The astronomical price that vintage and rare guitars reach at auction is understandably an incentive for fraudsters to release guitars with a faked history and aged parts and logos to suit. Guitar magazines don't go out of their way to deliberately mislead the reader. However April Fools gags occasionally backfire. In 1992, The Guitar Magazine published photographs of an unusual looking guitar, apparently a prototype of a 1958 Gibson model which never made it to production around the time that the Explorer and Firebird were being developed. The newly rediscovered Gibson 'Thunderbolt' looked a little like a Flying V with one leg reversed to make a Thunderbolt shape, black colour with two pickups and Tune-O-Matic bridge.

Perhaps the reader looking at the date of the April 1st Issue would have recognised the guitar for what it really was. Guitar magazine writer Dave Burrluck conceived the idea as an April Fools day joke and asked a guitar maker to mock up a 'Thunderbolt' from old parts. The Thunderbolt was seriously reviewed in the magazine and authenticated with a convincing history.

Even The Guitar Magazine didn't realise how far the joke would run until later in the year when another writer noticed a similar looking (real) guitar amongst a collection belonging to Rick Neilsen, guitarist with Cheap Trick. The guitar was apparently a real 'Gibson Thunderbolt', one of a kind and absolutely priceless, being a prototype. The Thunderbolt had even been reviewed in a quality UK magazine, and was attributed to Gibson by a highly respected journalist! As The Guitar Magazine isn't distributed in the states it's not difficult to imagine an unscrupulous US builder constructing a Thunderbolt from the picture in the magazine and selling it as an original. The flash of brilliance though is in the builder using the real looking review to sell it. Apparently Rick Neilsen took the gag firmly on the chin though it's not clear what kind of a battering his wallet may have suffered!

(Courtesy Dave Burrluck)

Attention Guitarists!

Recording the Guitar

Get a great sound onto tape

John Harris

156 pp • 244 x 172 mm • illustrated
ISBN 1 870775 45 7

★ Micing up vs DI for electric guitars
★ Mic positioning for acoustic guitars
★ Using effects to improve your sound
★ MIDI for guitarists
★ Sampling your guitar sound
★ Production tips and tricks

You'll know what it's like. You spend ages getting that great guitar sound and as soon as you put it on tape it sounds like a wet string flapping limply in the breeze.

Well here comes John Harris to the rescue. He calls on his many years of experience as a guitarist and recording engineer to bring you a collection of invaluable tips to help you get stunning results from your recordings.

He starts with setting up, strings, intonation and playing techniques. All these can affect the sound you ultimately put on to tape. Electric guitarists will learn when to mic up, when to DI (and when to do both!) and diagrams illustrate a range of different mic positions to coax the sweetest sounds from your acoustic.

John shows how different pre-amps – valve, transistor, digital – can be used for different sorts of music. And you'll find out how to put the finishing touches to your masterpiece with effects – compression, reverb, delay, gating, flange, chorus, harmonisers etc. etc. And don't believe MIDI is out of place in a guitarist's book. You'll find out about pedalboards, MIDI controllers, program switching and MIDI patchbays. And for real technofreaks there's a section on recording MIDI guitar, sequencers, and sampling .

The book is rounded off with tips on production techniques, like sound layering and tape tricks, and getting the final mix just right.

PC Publishing
Tel 01732 770893 • Fax 01732 770268 • email pcp@cix.compulink.co.uk
website http://www.pc-pubs.demon.co.uk

10

Identification

We all want to know as much about our guitars as possible, but how much information is available depends on the manufacturer and their record keeping. A guitar that retails for less than £400 often won't have much information other than the approximate date of manufacture. Large manufacturers such as Cort in South Korea make thousands of guitars each year. These are then shipped all over the globe to anyone with the money. If you want a range of guitars with your name on the headstock, phone 'em up and ask for a catalogue (minimum order is 500). Every guitar is identified by the serial number which is noted when the guitar is shipped, and if you are lucky the manufacturer might be able to trace the date of the shipment from the serial number. Details of materials, pickups and tremolo will have to be found in catalogues if possible

Many people write to guitar magazines asking for information along the lines of 'I have an Encore Classic which I bought second hand last year. Can you tell me when my guitar was made and what it is worth?' Usually these letters go unanswered because the information is too personal. The best place to find this information is from the distributor – the people that import and sell the guitar to shops on behalf of the maker

Dating old instruments

Guitar genealogy is a growing area of interest, particularly as the electric guitar is now over forty years old. Old or 'vintage' instruments have a higher resale value due to their perceived authenticity, and it follows that the older your guitar is, the more it might be worth. This is particularly true for guitars made more than 20 years ago. Before this point the guitar isn't yet ready for the 'vintage' market.

Most players like to know more about their own personal instrument, even if it's not to decide on its financial value. There are many well researched reference books on this subject which can help you to date your guitar, particularly if it's an American guitar from one of the famous manufacturers. As a last resort the only thing to do is contact the manufacturer directly. A list of distributors, manufacturers and their addresses is at the end of this book.

Be careful, guitar dating by serial number is a nightmare. For instance Gibson didn't rationalise their serial numbering until 1961, nine years after they began production of the Les Paul and three years after the 'classic' 1958 date for Les Paul Standards.

INFO

*F*ender has an Internet Web Page for dating its instruments: http:\\www.fender.com

Gibson SG guitar (courtesy of Gibson Guitar Corp.)

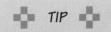
TIP

If you own a good example of an American instrument made in the middle – late seventies, the time to sell it will be after the millennium. Hold on to it, keep it as near factory condition, and above all don't customise!

INFO

George Gruhn's Vintage Guitar Shop in Nashville recently had a prototype Gibson Flying 'V' for sale at $100,000.

Fender have a more consistent serial numbering policy but duplications are frequent. In other words up to three different Fender guitars can share the same serial number. Modern instruments (post 1975) are much easier to date by serial number as both Fender and Gibson revised their serial number format to incorporate a date code.

However finding the serial number can be troublesome. Old Fender instruments have a serial number at the bottom of the neck, actually inside the heel joint. So before dating the guitar you have to take apart an instrument possibly worth thousands of pounds! Gibson guitars are easier, the serial number is stamped on the back of the headstock. If your Gibson guitar doesn't have a serial number it's either a priceless 1952 Les Paul Gold Top or a fake. Both instances would have me calling Nashville for clarification.

Gibson date codes (post 1975)

One two digit number is used to indicate the year of manufacture, followed by a six figure number between 100000 and 200000

99XXXXXX	1975
00XXXXXX	1976
06XXXXXX	1977

After 1977 Gibson again changed their serial number format to include both the year and day of the year. This system remains with a few exceptions until today.

Year,Day,Day,Day,Year,Plant,Plant,Plant

Of course the manufacturer's serial number wasn't intended to be used as a device for accurately determining the production date of your guitar, particularly for instruments before 1975. Many other things have to be taken into account such as fittings, finish and even the physical dimensions of the instrument. The high value of 'vintage' guitars at auction has brought a number of faked instruments onto the market and it would be foolish for anyone considering purchasing a vintage instrument to rely on the serial number alone as proof that the guitar is what it seems.

'Custom shop' and other high end instruments

You don't have to buy a production guitar. Custom shop instruments and artist models are available from every manufacturer. For some people the ultimate guitar is a 'custom shop' instrument, built to your own specifications. Of course the price of these instruments is significantly higher than regular production instruments but you will have a unique 'couture' instrument, tailor made to suit you and your music. The motive for owning a custom shop guitar is often in the desire to own an instrument that few, if any other people, will have.

But before shelling out for the deposit it's worth thinking hard about what you need. For many people the finish of the guitar is very important. 'Harley Davidson' and 'Western' guitars with gear sticks and cow horns look great but are unlikely to be very practical or very easy to play, or sound good in the end. In fact some guitar builders actually try and talk people out of a custom shop guitar because they believe that the customer will get better value for money from a well chosen production guitar. On the other hand the major manufacturers have plenty to gain from high value, high profile custom shop instruments which carry as much advertising as they do personal satisfaction. So is the satisfaction you are after in the final feel of the instrument or in the name at the top of the headstock?

Aged guitars

As guitars become increasingly valuable, the desire to own a 'relic' is reaching fever point. Classic American guitars such as a good condition 1960's Les Paul Standard easily fetch upwards of £8,000. Prices like these mean that a comfortable, played in twenty year old Fender Strat is no longer the kind of thing you want to leave propped up against a chair in a pub during the break between sets.

New guitars don't have the cachet of an older guitar, so Fender have a line of custom shop 'aged' Stratocasters and Telecasters. These guitars are artificially aged with cigarette burns and battery acid to make a brand new guitar appear as if it were a well played twenty year old model. They are absolutely indistinguishable from the real thing, right down to the rust on the bridge pieces. Unfortunately they are also twice the price of a regular Fender Standard Stratocaster.

Relic Fender Telecaster® but at an up-to-date price!

11

Gigging and recording

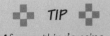
All that hard work, all those hours practising, all the money spent on buying equipment. Everything you do to become a guitar player is all about making it work live. The payback is standing on stage and feeling that applause – nothing comes close. To gig successfully you need to know a little more than it's possible to discover just by playing in your bedroom or in the garage. The law of sod applies itself more successfully on stage than anywhere else. So if something's going to go wrong, it'll go usually go wrong at the gig, not the soundcheck. This is a pity because that's what the soundcheck is for. This in itself is a perfect example of the law of sod in full effect.

Sound on stage

There are two sorts of performances you make when you play your guitar: private and public. You do a private performance every time you pick up the guitar to practise or to record. The guitar sound you are most familiar with is the one you produce in this kind of environment. Whenever you play live at gig level you make a public performance. The important part is that your public sound is often completely different to your private sound, and you might not notice the difference. This is because your audience is standing a few feet, or a hundred yards away. They hear a different sound from your amp. Therefore, the most successful guitar sound is the one that sounds good to both you and your audience.

Creating a good public sound involves a little experimentation and the application of a couple of scientific facts. Treble and bass frequencies project and disperse in different ways. To even these, out take your guitar off the stage and put it either on a chair or a stand, a beer crate will do. The important thing is to get the speaker to about waist height. If you use a stack (two 4 x12 cabs) experiment with unplugging the bottom cab to get the same visual impact but with a better sound. Many pro bands use a combination of speaker cabs and a speaker emulator. The Front Of House engineer will use both feeds to create one good sound. This is how experienced live sound engineers such as Paul King create mix guitar for Terrorvision; 'The sound of a speaker can change from one night to the next. If you have a speaker and a speaker emulator I would mike and DI at the same time.'

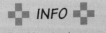

INFO

Backline is the collection of instrument amps, effects and other equipment that the band uses on stage at the gig. The PA engineer uses microphones to feed the backline to the front-of-house mixing desk with a split feed to the monitor desk and amps.

View from the stage at the
Reading festival

Stage volume levels at festivals and major venues are sometimes surprisingly quiet. This obviously depends on the band, Metallica and Oasis
for instance are well known for deafeningly loud backline, but many
bands try and keep volume levels down as much as possible. If this sort of
discipline is available in your band you'll find a better sound, especially at
club and pub levels where the sound engineer is often fighting against the
backline to get the singer heard. Low volume levels on stage also help
keep the band tight and produce a better performance. You'll always get a
better sound if your equipment isn't working too hard. So choose an amp
that's up to the job. Although practice amps are sometimes great in the
studio, it's rare for one to make it to the stage.

Amps for gigging and recording

Venue	Maximum watts	Speakers	e.g.
Bedroom practice	10 W RMS	1 x 6.5 inch	Park PG10Mk2
School concert	25 W per channel	2 x 8 inch stereo amp	Peavey Transfex 208
Pub or night-club	60 W	2 x 10 inch	Laney GC60C
College tour	65 W per channel (130 W)	2 x 12	Marshall Valvestate VS265R
Concert tour	2 x 100 W heads (200 W)	16 x 12 inch (two stacks)	2 x Marshall JCM900
Arena tour	4 x 100 W heads (400 W)	32 x 12 inch (four stacks)	4 x Mesa Boogie Dual Rectifier Solo Head
Pro recording	30 W	2 x 12 inch	Matchless John Jorgenson

Most people can't afford the luxury of different amps for gigging and
recording, but try to avoid selling your amps as you move up the chain.

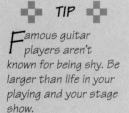

✦ TIP ✦

Famous guitar players aren't known for being shy. Be larger than life in your playing and your stage show.

The money you'll make on resale is as nothing compared to the pain you'll feel when your first amp becomes a classic twenty years after you sold it. And it's useful to have a selection of amps to use in the studio, whatever stage of playing you are at.

Getting a guitar 'sound'

Every time you pickup up a magazine you read about somebody else's 'sound'. Some people go a long way to emulate the sound of a particular guitar player that they love, even buying the same gear or learning to play the same way. Getting your own sound is much more important than getting somebody else's. Your own sound is all about who you are as a guitar player, it's like your speaking voice. The character and individualism of your own sound is more likely to appear just when you don't expect it, probably when you've forgotten about trying to get it. Here are a few pointers towards helping you make your own statement.

* Be yourself. An Epiphone Slash or a Jackson Randy Rhoads is still somebody else's guitar.
* Take one small part of your playing, something that you do really well like a riff or a phrase, anything that comes naturally. Take this one part and practise it until it comes into everything you do.
* Invest some time in examining your on-stage sound. Really make sure that your audience knows it's you that's playing.

Playing live

Playing live can be terrifying, even for the most experienced player. The key to conquering fear (which after all is based on the unknown) is planning and rehearsal, bringing as much as possible under your control. The most important thing to do is to learn the material that you'll be playing.

Stadium backline Marshall guitar stack

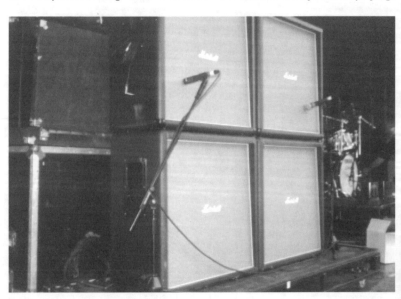

Don't rely on your adrenaline to bring it off. If you know your parts backward you'll cope with anything else that might happen.

Many bands organise 'production rehearsals' a couple of evenings before the gig. This means using a different rehearsal studio and playing the songs in gig order - even videotaping your set. Be prepared for a shock but it'll do you good!

Make sure your gear is OK, change your strings a couple of days before the gig (but after the production rehearsal). Really get that on-stage sound sorted out. This might even involve going to rehearsals a few hours early to experiment with your live sound and get it right. Make sure you have spare batteries, leads and anything else you have spares for. Don't forget extension 'trailing sockets' because there'll never be enough mains outlets at the gig. and don't forget your RCD (residual current detector) to make sure that your gear is safe.

Successful gigging

* Learn the material! Don't worry about being 'over-rehearsed' (it rarely happens!).

* Plan a production rehearsal.

* Maintain your kit!

* Sort your sound out

* Take spares.

* Keep yourself safe!

Going to tape

Demo tapes are vital for your songwriting and for getting gigs – maybe even a record deal. So before too long you'll be recording yourself, or someone else will want to record either you or your band. This will probably be in somebody's bedroom to begin with, but inevitably you'll find yourself visiting a large recording complex one day, and probably won't ever want to leave.

This feeling usually lasts until shortly after your second album when all of a sudden the idea of visiting a studio begins to feel far too much like going to work. At this point the record company start mumbling about 'that difficult third album,' and before you know it you are dropped for 'losing the plot' But that's show business.

If you have a band you'll already know about getting a good guitar sound and working with other musicians to make music long before you ever put microphone to speaker. The surprising part is that's really all you need to know. Everything else is somebody else's job. It's the engineers role to get your sound on tape or disc as close to the original as possible. It's the producers role to direct the session and make sure that the record is going in the right direction for the band and/or for the recording company, depending on who is doing the hiring.

Rigging for the studio in a band situation is almost the same as rigging for a gig. The difference is that in the studio your audience is:

* Probably not drunk or under the influence of mind expanding drugs (depending on the band of course).
* A lot more critical (depending on genre of music, age of expected market etc.).

Recording the guitar can be compared to passing everything you do under a large and expensive audio microscope. Things that would never occur to you as problems will jump out at just the wrong time. That time is usually about 3am on a Monday morning when the chances of getting hold of a set of mandolin strings are closer to zero than a polar bear's backside.

The industry term for identifying and removing these problems before you get to the studio is 'routineering'. All this means is that you take yourself and your gear into a rehearsal studio for a couple of nights to examine very closely what you do. As a guitar player it's easy to do this on your own. Take yourself through each song at listening level (not gig level) and track down every pop and click from your noisy wah pedal through to the interference from the taxi company down the road. Then fix these problems on your own time. Simply put, small things that don't seem at all important suddenly become magnified out of all proportion in the studio.

Look at it this way. Your guitar cable costs £5. Studio time costs in the region of £25 per hour. If your guitar lead is bad it might crackle. On stage this might not matter. In the studio you could spend two hours laying down a gob smackingly fantastic solo when right at the end your guitar lead spoils the whole thing. Result is a missed take, a pissed off producer, your reputation down the swanee and £50 (at least) of wasted studio time.

Things to take to your first session:

* Spare strings.
* Spare batteries.
* Spare leads (all sorts including MIDI).
* Extra media (floppy disks or video tapes etc.).

Things to leave at home:

* Your mum and dad.
* Beer.
* Your girlfriend.
* Your (ahem) manager.

Why is taking your girlfriend to the studio *such* a bad idea?

Believe it or not, watching a band work in a studio is about as exciting as watching somebody play a video game. There's no fun in sitting in a smelly room full of people intently pushing buttons and muttering about '.. is the MIDI receive channel set right, or is local off?' Truth is it's really frustrating because you'll never hear the whole track how its meant to be, just annoying little bits before someone winds back. And it's no use voicing any opinions. Therefore, unless your idea of a good night out involves 'popping out to the shop for a packet of fags and some biscuits' you are better off at home in front of the TV.

Getting sandwiches is the teaboy (or girls) job anyway. He or she happily accepts the role of being sent out for sandwiches in the hope that one day the producer will meet with an unhappy accident involving a piece of thin rope, a large and heavy object and a sharp knife. Then Teaboy magically gets promoted to Producer. This is actually how it works by the way. Difficult to believe that simply popping to the shops to buy sandwiches for your partner might affect somebody else's career prospects isn't it? Welcome to the world of studio politics - another reason why you don't want to hang around.

If you are a girlfriend or boyfriend of somebody in the band, the only advantage you might see in hanging around the studio is the chance of meeting/adopting/enjoying close personal contact with someone much more famous than the group of no-hopers you came in with. This usually leads to the same thing as before with the sandwiches etc. but generally you'll have a comfier sofa to sit on – and maybe some fruit.

Hints for people hanging around in studios

Don't ever sit in the producer's chair.

Ask before you eat anything just in case it's been provided for the prima donna lead singer who simple can't perform without a packet of his favourite chocolate biscuits close to hand.

Be prepared to be very bored.

Take a magazine and don't complain when somebody steals it.

Don't nick the teaboy's job.

Recording tips

It's the engineer's job to put a microphone in front of your amp, get the sound to tape etc., but make yourself appear a bit less of a dim bulb by nodding your head when you hear the following things:

Q 'Is the reverb on your amp turned on?'
This is a cue to turn the reverb off because somebody in the control room doesn't like the sound of it. If it's your sound and you are paying for the session somehow then insist that you leave it on. If the producer has hired you, apologise and turn it off.

Usually reverb is added to recordings after the session. This enables the producer to choose the type and balance without fighting with your amp reverb. If the reverb is a vital part of your sound (an unusual event) then it's OK to leave it on. Usually it's better to turn it off and ask for some reverb in your headphones instead.

Q 'Which speaker?'
The engineer will ask this if you have a cab with more than one speaker. If the engineer is 'close miking' the microphone will be placed next to just one speaker and the engineer is asking you which sounds best. If you don't know, play a few bars and let the engineer decide. Then note it with tape for next time.

Q 'What do you want in your headphones'
This very much depends on where you are at with the track. If it's early on and you are laying a rhythm part over some drums and bass then all you'll need is drums and bass. However if it's a frilly solo over the end then you might want a general mix to get the feel of the track. Generally it's best to have as little as possible in your headphones as you need to concentrate on your part. Cue parts are drums, bass and vocal. If in doubt ask for cue parts first and then add more later. A confusing headphone mix is worse than anything.

Recording happens in stages depending on the band, the producer's routine, type of music being recorded, technology available, etc. For a straightforward song the band will usually set up as they would for a gig. Each member is miked or connected to the mixing desk and tape machine and the song is recorded as the band plays the whole song from beginning to end.

The song might need to be played a number of times, each 'take' recorded so the producer can make a judgement later on about which feels best. The chosen take is then the basis for the rest of the recording including any overdubs, additional parts, MIDI instruments etc. The tape tracks that have been recorded are called 'guide tracks' and won't usually be included in the final mix. They are simply there as reference. Later on each band member will re-record their own parts again. It's the re-recording that is used in the final mix.

You don't have to sit in another room to record guitar – why not use the lines that every studio has between control room and live room to connect your guitar and amp? This suits many situations, especially if your part is complex and you don't have many guitar effects to worry about. On the other hand a lot of players use the dynamic of guitar and amp to enhance their playing.

If you are sitting in the control room make sure you can see the track time indicator. This is usually on a TV screen either above or in the desk. If your track has MIDI backing there will be a PC monitor with a Cubase or E-magic arrange window somewhere. What you are looking for is a way to know where you are in a track. The song position indicator will show you where you are with a vertical line that moves as the track plays.

If you know where you are it's easy to be ready for the drop in or whatever the producer has in mind.

Recording the guitar

✦ *INFO* ✦

*C*heck out the book 'Recording the Guitar' by John Harris, available from this publisher.

That's a big subject, worth a book on its own. I get loads of letters asking the best way to record the guitar and there is no quick answer. The only thing to say is that it's a lot easier to get guitars onto a record now than it ever was. Thanks to DSP and multi-effects you don't anymore have to drag four tons of amp and cab into a studio. On the other hand Noel Gallagher uses more Marshall equipment on stage than several pub bands put together. On the third hand I knew at least one 'name' band who hid behind a stack of dry ice while a couple of guitar multi-effects did the business in the wings, making the act of packing up and going home a lot easier.

So the answer is - there's no answer. But like the man climbing the mountain, it's a lot easier if someone goes ahead with a torch. So here are a few tips to keep you going till you reach the top.

Recording with a four tracker

Most players start recording with a cassette based four track. Four tracking has the advantage of using dead cheap media (cassette tape) meaning loads of demos for not much money.

Getting your guitar to tape:

* Use a compressor to enable you to get as much sound on tape as possible without distortion.
* Stay away from huge reverb pads that just get lost in a mix.
* Remember that the guitar occupies the middle range of frequencies, just about the same range that the snare drum also uses. So plan your mix to give the maximum space to each instrument.

At demo stage most results come from multi-effects, such as the Boss GT-5 or Zoom 1010, both of which offer a perfectly respectable guitar sound at varying prices. If you must use your amp then bodge a patch cord from the headphone socket. Don't use the extension speaker socket or you'll blow your four tracker up. It is perfectly all right to use stomp boxes straight into the four track, but watch the gain from heavy metal type pedals. Try using your stomp box delays and reverbs as four track effects.

Microphones are easy to use but getting a truly pro sound is difficult without the premium quality microphone amps, compressors etc. that don't come included with portastudios. Unfortunately using a microphone and portastudio for guitar sounds at this level probably won't give you the results you are looking for. At the four track stage I'd stick to multi-effects for guitar sounds and use a microphone just for vocals.

Session playing

If making regular money as a guitar player is what you want, then session playing is what you need to do. Session players turn up for anything at anytime and play whatever the producer wants them to. To do this you need to live in or around London. You could base yourself around another major city but make sure it's one that has a thriving (and I mean thriving) music scene. A good choice might be Manchester or Glasgow, anywhere that's more than three hours fast driving away from the next nearest major population centre. After that you'll need a reputation.

Getting a good reputation involves being a great player, having a flexible nature and lot's of hard work – in about a 20%, 30%, 50% order. I know that twenty years ago I wanted two things – money and a Fender Stratocaster. I thought I was good enough to be a player and nothing at all could convince me otherwise.

In the end I left school early, took myself off to London and through a friend of a friend (both music college students) I got a break then got what I wanted – a job playing the guitar in a reeasonable famous band. Because I didn't know anything I thought that my playing would be enough to carry me through. It was for a short while but when the competition got tough I realised I didn't have two things that any successful player needs; a background and a reputation.

I didn't have a background because, although I had plenty of self confidence, I didn't have anything to prove it. In a business like the music business talk is cheap and proof is needed. All I had was me going 'I can do that!' What I needed was the one thing that everyone told me I didn't need – a guitar education, preferably from a fairly heavyweight institution.

On the other hand getting a reputation as a guitar player relies on getting results – preferably in the form of a featuring role on a pretty successful record. With one of those under your belt other people can go 'you know him – he played that solo on that record', bingo – much easier to get a booking.

Your best start is through contact with other musicians. If you are still at school then aim for a London music school. Once there don't leave, grit your teeth and come out with your diploma. If music school isn't your bag then leave your job, buy some gear and beg, beg and beg again to join somebody's band. Once in London don't stop playing and asking until people start paying for your services.

The gap between arriving in town and making a living is usually about seven years. The key to it all is being in the right place at the right time and above all knowing the right people. For session musicians this means belonging to a reputable agency or being a producer's pet (first call for just one successful producer). Actually getting an agent who'll get you any work is a lifetime's job in itself.

Aspiring session musicians need as much in their arsenal as possible

Learn to sight read music and rhythm charts

Buy the best and most reliable gear possible

Buy an estate car to take all that stuff around with you

Buy a fax machine

Get a mobile phone

Get a London flat

Get a sympathetic partner

Buy a very good pension plan.

Touring abroad

Guitars on aircraft

Many people wonder how to get their guitar safely on board an aircraft, and horror stories abound of people who find their precious instrument in pieces at the end of the flight. With a little forethought and by asking the right questions it is possible to avoid damaging your instrument, and even ensure that the baggage handlers take special care.

Touring bands

Bands with many items of equipment that need to travel with them must make special arrangements to have the equipment loaded onto the plane. Because bands at this level usually have their equipment flight cased already, worrying about damage isn't so much of a problem . However you will still need to pass all these cases through customs. The customs people will need to see an official document called a carnet. This is a list of all the equipment in the cases, right down to leads and floppy disks. The list notes make, model, serial number and even value, so the customs men can ensure that what is going out of the country is the same as what's coming back in. The purpose of this is to stop people taking out a cheap copy guitar and bringing back an expensive original in the same case. Gear transported this way is stored in a standard container for travel in the ordinary hold of the aircraft.

Solo musicians and ordinary travellers

The best thing to do is ask that your equipment is put in the 'loose load' compartment. This is usually Hold 5 on a Jumbo jet and is the place reserved for pets, artworks and other valuable items that can't be carried in the passenger compartment but still need care. Hold 5 is the only heated hold so if your guitar is in a thin case in one of the other holds it could be damaged as the temperature easily drops to well below freezing.

Obviously this doesn't matter to your underwear or anything in an insulated suitcase, but guitars are temperature sensitive and don't react at all well to extremes of cold or heat. Items that are bound for loose loading are carried onto the aircraft by hand and strapped into the loose load area individually. This is the safest way to transport your guitar in an aircraft.

Incidentally, all short haul domestic flights are loose load, although the compartment may not be heated. In this case request that your guitar is stowed last, in other words on top of all the other items. Absolute safety isn't guaranteed but it's the best option. Telephone the carrier before your trip to arrange for your guitar to be stored in the loose load area.

Aircraft holds are pressurised but unheated (except for loose load as described above). This means that temperatures can easily go below -30 degrees C, far below freezing point. This is why you hear about stow-aways freezing to death. If you are planning to put your guitar in the hold, even the loose load hold, it's wise to take a few precautions. Don't detune the guitar, you need to ensure even tension along the neck. Remove all pressurised containers such as polish etc. For long flights wrap the guitar in soft cloth or any insulating material. Lock the case and put *FRAGILE* stickers prominently on the case. Attach a sticker or label with your name, flight number and destination address (and telephone number) just in case.

Cabin baggage

If your guitar is very valuable and without a flightcase you might be able to arrange for the guitar to travel with you in the passenger compartment. On British Airways flights, each passenger is allowed 6k of cabin baggage (9k for Business Class passengers). Most guitars weigh much more than this so special arrangements must be made if you want to carry your guitar with you. Don't try and stow it in the overhead locker, it won't fit and you'll annoy the other passengers.

Guitars can be carried in the passenger compartment in two ways. Some players even pay for a seat for the instrument. (not as uncommon as it sounds). The seat is charged at full rate although no one was available to tell me whether the accompanying musician was entitled to the spare in flight meal or alcohol! The only other way is to approach the cabin crew in the right manner (this means politely and not two minutes before take off) and ask if there is any chance that the instrument might be stowed in the passenger compartment wardrobe. Most aircraft (especially long haul jumbos) have wardrobes for cabin crew and passengers, and if the aircraft isn't full and you smile sweetly and offer your autograph, you could save yourself a lot of money. Of course if you bundle up to the check-in desk with five minutes to go and demand that your Les Paul occupies the seat next to you, you won't get very far at all. Be charming instead.

Again it's a very good idea to phone the carrier before you arrive at the airport to advise that you are carrying an expensive item. You'll find that the airline is very happy to help and will do all they can. Of course if you wind them up you might find your priceless '54 Strat at the bottom of a pile of suitcases but that's your own fault.

Finally (and 'off the record' according to British Airways Cabin Crew) if it's an empty aeroplane and there's plenty of room the cabin crew might simply let you strap it in the next seat, but it's not guaranteed.

Damage

If your instrument is damaged and you want the money to buy a new one you'll have to do two things. Firstly prove that you took all reasonable precautions to avoid damage. This means proof that you asked for loose load etc. Secondly you'll need a valuation (before you travel). This can be a receipt or a valuation from a respected shop etc. If you notice damage don't leave the airport without telling the carrier and getting the right claim forms. At this point certainly complain loudly because the last thing the carrier wants is a noisy complainant. Keep calm, but be firm – and take pictures.

12

Trouble

Trouble must come one day and as a guitar player surely it will. Boy Scout or Boy Band the message is the same. Be prepared, even if it just means carrying your BT Chargecard for those 4 am motorway station blues.

Top ten gear and guitar problems

Feedback

What is feedback? There are two principal sorts; resonant and microphonic. Resonant feedback is the good sort, the kind that can keep your guitar note sustaining for ever or help you sound like the millennium mothership just landed inside your amp.

Resonant feedback

This kind of feedback is generated by the strings of your guitar and the air spaces in your guitar. Whenever you play your guitar through an amp your speakers are moving air at the same frequency as the strings on your guitar are vibrating. If your strings can sense the moving air they'll want to keep on vibrating, you no longer have to provide the energy to move the string, the strings now doing that for itself, through the amp. This kind of feedback is usually welcome.

Any guitar will feed back but because the ability of the guitar to do this is helped by the amount of air inside the guitar, bigger guitars and especially guitars with air holes such as semi-solid guitars are much more likely to feedback. If you use high gain distortion pedals or a compressor you'll have more feedback as the high gain pedal will make your amp much more sensitive and the compressor will turn your guitar up when the note would otherwise be dying away.

Microphonic feedback

Feedback usually isn't a problem. The right sort of feedback is a great musical tool which is exclusive to the guitar, for many people it is the sound of the guitar. Can you imagine a sampler feeding back rich harmonic overtones? – nope! But there is another sort of feedback which is unpleasant and very difficult to control. 'Microphonic feedback' is easy to recognise as a really horrible car alarm style howl and whistle that seems

TIP

If you don't want resonant feedback stop up the air holes inside your guitar with foam to stop the air moving (this also changes the sound of your guitar) or use a graphic equaliser to 'notch out' the troublesome frequencies.

to come out of nowhere, especially frustrating as it will often happen at a much lower volume than the good sort. The problem is caused by a broken or badly made pickup. After a while some pickups – especially budget ones – begin to fall apart inside. The case or a pole piece might shake loose or part of the coil may detach from the other windings. When this happens the pickup develops the ability to induce (cause a signal) by itself, it doesn't need the guitar string any more. The amount of trouble this can cause is very small – until you add a high gain device which takes every scratch and scrape, every minute noise from your pickup and boosts it maybe by 100 db. All of a sudden your malfunctioning pickup becomes a one man band as it literally turns in on itself !

The only way to fix this properly is to have your pickup repaired or potted in wax or plastic. This can be even more expensive than buying a new pickup which is often a better option. The answer to the question 'is it worth replacing my pickups?' is often yes. New pickups will breathe new life and character into your guitar.

Checklist

Invest in quality pickups

Consider replacing the pickups on a budget guitar

Noisy potentiometer

The carbon or conductive plastic track inside the volume and tone controls on your guitar isn't indestructible. As they wear out they become crackly and scratchy, producing interference as you turn the control. The solution to this is either to spray the inside of the potentiometer with a residue free cleaner or to remove and replace altogether. Spray cleaning is a short term option, if the inside of the pot has become so dirty that you need to clean it then corrosion is already happening – which means replacing it soon anyway.

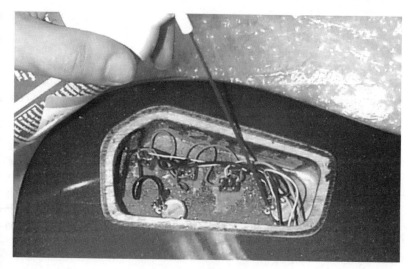

Use contact cleaner to remove dirt from a volume or tone pot

Replacing a pot isn't difficult and spares are cheap – just a pound or so for a brand new control. Potentiometer values vary from model to model. To determine the value of your pot look closely at the back for a value stamped into the metal, or contact the manufacturer or distributor.

Checklist

Regularly use contact cleaner

Know how to change a broken pot

Interference

Interference from hecklers is something you have to live with. Interference from TV, CB and other radio frequency emissions is avoidable (or at least tameable). The solution is good grounding. Part of the reason that the PAF pickup is so famous is that it was designed as a noise reduction device, the great sound just came along as part of the deal. PAF pickups reject noise because the earth ground is connected to the screen of the cable from the pickup to the volume control. This is then carried around the guitar body by conductive paint or shielding which is connected in turn to the guitar cord and so to the amp and to ground via the earth pin in the wall socket. Many guitars feature a string ground meaning a short wire from the back of the volume pot to the bridge and so to the strings. When you touch the strings you connect to ground through your feet and so complete the circuit.

Shielding protects the guitar electronics from interference by providing a route which carries unwanted noise away to earth. So noise can happen if one of two things go wrong.

1 If the guitar electronics aren't properly shielded interference will happen
2 If the shield isn't connected to ground there's no place for the noise to go

To remove noise from your guitar it must be shielded and the shielding must be connected to ground. Shielding your guitar from interference usually involves using conductive paint or tape to make a virtual 'cage' protecting the control cavity inside the guitar. Ensure there is a good connection between the cage and the metal cap covering the back of your volume and tone pots. There must also be a good connection between the back of the pots and the ground connection of your jack socket. The object is to ensure that the control cavity is surrounded by an metal box. Radio and Electro Magnetic interference will be dissipated by the box instead of being picked up by the 'hot' connections inside the guitar. If this cage is connected to the screen of your guitar cable, and if the cable is connected to earth then interference will go directly to where it wants to go – earth – instead of buzzing around your guitar and causing problems.

The amount of shielding you need depends on where you live and whether you play around the country. If you experience strong interference that appears to happen only from one local Taxi firm you might have a case to put to your local council.

Checklist

Interference is caused by poor shielding

Use good quality guitar cables

Invest time in ensuring that your guitar is properly protected

Learn how to use a continuity meter

Buzzing open strings

Buzzing at the first fret under an open string is caused by a poorly cut top nut. the nut will need to be replaced and cut to suit the neck profile. Buzzing at the fifth and seventh fret is usually caused by poor neck relief, in this case truss rod adjustment will be necessary. Sometimes buzzing is also the result poor neck pitch. This is especially true if the buzzing happens at the 14th fret or higher while the action around the third fret seems to be high.

Checklist

Have your guitar professionally set up

Always go carefully with DIY repairs

Effects of humidity and central heating

The golden rule to storing guitars is 'Never store a guitar where you wouldn't be comfortable yourself.' This includes keeping your guitar away from extremes of heat, cold and humidity. Central heating usually isn't a problem with modern guitars. If you have an older guitar, particularly an acoustic guitar that might need special attention then leave the guitar in its case when not being played.

When storing a guitar for long periods of time don't be tempted to remove or slacken the strings as the tension supplied by the strings is necessary to keep the guitar neck from becoming twisted. Cover the strings with a soft clean cloth and leave a pocket humidifier in the case to attract moisture away from the guitar:

Checklist

Keep old guitars in cases

Never detune a guitar prior to long term storage

Invest in a pocket humidifier

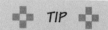

TIP

Sometimes taxi and pizza delivery firms operate unlicensed radio equipment that transmits on radio frequencies other than those which the government has allowed for this purpose. In this case (particularly if you have invested large amounts of money in studio equipment) you might be able to remove the interference at source.

Rattle and odd tones at bridge

Just like the guitar nut, the guitar bridge saddles may wear and need some attention. A typical symptom of this is odd halftones and rattles from the wound strings as they pass over the saddles. Sometimes this is difficult to hear and is often more evident when the electric guitar is played acoustically – not plugged in. A worn saddle often needs nothing more than a little attention with a small fine round file. The depth of cut isn't as crucial as nut work as the bridge can be raised or lowered to compensate. The width of the slot is crucial though, the last thing you want is a string that's slipping from side to side:

Checklist

Check saddle problems with guitar unplugged

Invest in good set of smooth round files

Strings that go out of tune when using the tremolo

Floating tremolo systems can be just a stable as complex Floyd Rose style trems with string clamps and locking nut. The object is to enable the string to glide through the nut and bridge easily enough to enable the tremolo to drop or raise pitch while ensuring that the string can return to the same place each time.

At the bridge

Spend some time on the tremolo block. Use a round file to remove any burrs from the string guides inside the block. Ensure that the ball end is able to sit neatly inside the tremolo block, if necessary use Fender 'Bullet' strings which dispense with the traditional ball end in favour of shaped brass string ends designed to sit securely inside the block. Smooth the bridge saddles and all pivot points. If necessary enlarge the string hole slightly, especially for the wound strings. A little lubricating oil inside the block will help to ensure the strings return to the same place each time. Examine the string claw that anchors the tremolo springs to the back of the guitar. Spring tension is important, adjust the spring claw by screwing or unscrewing the retaining screws. The object is to balance the tremolo so that the bridge is just above the top of the guitar, not sitting on top of it when the tremolo is at rest. If necessary remove or add springs to the tremolo. Experiment with different springs if you like, they'll make a big difference to how the tremolo feels and reacts.

At the nut

Carefully smooth the nut slots and add a little graphite based lubricating oil to each slot.

At the tuning machines

Stretch each string so that no extra movement is available when the string is tuned to pitch. Ensure that the windings on the tuning machines do not overlap and that there is at least five windings on the 1st, 2nd and 3rd tuning machines. You could consider investing in a set of Sperzel locking tuning machines which will not allow the string to move and do not need tools to unlock. The tuning peg is retracted slightly into the tuner by a wheel on the rear of the machine.

When should I change my guitar strings?

This very much depends on how often you play, the way you play and the weight or gauge of the strings you use. Every guitar string will break eventually, it's just a matter of time. The important part is knowing when the string is about to break. A metal string is subjected to abrasion, corrosion and fatigue. Each of these factors on its own is a hazard – together they add unpredictability to the list of problems. To avoid the unpredictable nature of string breakage follow these tips:

Checklist

Always use a complete set of strings, don't just change the one that's broken.

Add a spot of light oil to the bridge saddle, just before you tune the string for the first time. This forms a corrosion resistant layer between the string and metal bridge while adding additional lubrication. Only do this at string change with a new string, any other time the corrosion will already have started.

Always wipe the strings with a cotton cloth (not a yellow duster) after playing to remove moisture from the windings. Remember to wipe under the strings.

Make trimming wound strings the last thing you do after changing and tuning the entire set.

The frequency with which you change strings is much more personal. Session musicians need the sound of fresh strings for the studio and so are likely to change strings whenever their sound becomes degraded by the worn strings. A player who plays on stage is more likely to regard the possibility of string breakage as more of a problem but will know that a day old set of strings will stay in tune better than a set an hour old. Generally speaking if you play at home two or three times a week and rehearse with your band once a week you should change your strings at least once a month.

Fault finding a broken guitar cable

Sometimes a guitar cable will appear to work and then stop for no reason. Or the lead will work if you wrap it around a strap button or if you stand on it. In cases like these the problem is that the copper conductors inside the guitar lead have broken. By 'kinking' the cable it's possible to temporarily remake the connection which is broken again as soon as the cable is released. Before you rip apart a suspect cable it is a good idea to establish exactly where the fault is. Buy a brand new cable and try the guitar again. If the fault is still there then check the jack socket in your guitar and amp or effects (see flow diagram). If the fault disappears you have a broken cable. Don't throw it away, find the break and make a patch cable from the rest.

Inner core to tip

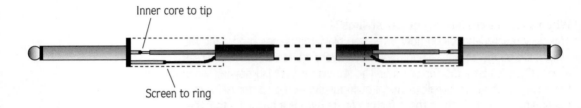

Screen to ring

Connections for a mono patch cable.

If your lead has professional barrel connectors, unscrew each barrel and check for breaks at in the plug. If all seem OK then the break is somewhere inside the cable. Plug the lead into a working amp and put your finger on the tip of the plug. You should hear a buzz. If not work along the lead 'kinking' as you go until you find the place where if you kink the lead you hear the guitar again. Mark an inch or so closer to the amp with tape then unplug the lead from the amp and cut the cable before the tape. You now have one good piece of cable and one bad piece. With luck the longer piece will be the good one. If not, measure 15 – 20 mm back along the bad cable and cut this piece out as well. Strip the end of the good piece and plug the cable into the amp. You will hear a buzz if you touch the bare inner connectors and nothing if you touch the screen. Finally attach a new jack plug to the good piece of cable and use as a patch or tuner lead.

Sometimes you might need to know if your lead is bad but you don't have access to an amp. For situations like this it's easy to rig a very simple continuity tester from a torch lamp and a battery.

What do I do If . . . ?

I break a string?
If your guitar is in tune.. keep going. It looks dead cool and you'll get brownie points from the rest of the band. If you guitar plunges out of tune then turn down and mime (it happens!) or grab another from your tech. Quick changing guitars on stage is simple if you work it out before-hand. Take your guitar off with your right hand and put the new one on with your left. If you don't have a tech or a spare guitar there's nothing for it but to abort and fit another one.

My lead is broken?
Keep a spare with your amp and unplug the lead from the amp first. Then plug the new lead in the guitar and check your tuner. If the tuner is OK then the new lead is OK too. Connect all your effects and plug into the amp last of all to avoid bangs and clicks while the singer is doing his solo spot.

I walk on stage, plug in and get no sound!
Listen to me very carefully. Is your guitar volume turned all the way up? It's a simple but horribly common mistake (grin).

Check the obvious things first. Is there power going to your amp? The easiest way to do this is to walk to the plug and see that it is still connected to the wall and to your amp. If this is all OK look carefully at your effects and make sure that they are all connected and are powered up. Then make sure your guitar is turned up. No good? Take the effects out and plug the guitar direct into the amp. If you still can't hear anything check that the lead is good by unplugging the guitar and touching the bare tip of the jack plug with your finger. If all is well you'll hear a loud buzz. If you don't hear a buzz unplug all your effects and keep trying until you do. If you have a guitar lead plugged directly into your amp, and you know that the lead is OK because your bass player used it but you don't hear anything then your amp has a problem. The trick is to eliminate all the variables first, then move on from there.

No sound panic checklist

Is the power getting to your amp?

Check that all your effects are connected up.

Make sure your guitar is turned up

Plug the guitar direct into the amp to bypass the effects

Try another lead

I think my guitar effects are broken?
Have they all got batteries in them? Plug a lead into the input and use the footswitch. If you don't get a red light then the battery is dead or missing, replace with one of the fresh batteries you always keep handy. .If the battery is good the problem is most likely to be with the patch cables. Replace with the spare ones you always carry in your trunk (grin). If the effect still will not work then it's not something you'll be able to fix tonight anyway (and didn't you think something was wrong when you checked your gear before you left home?)

I Need a longer guitar cable and there's a spare speaker cable in my bag.
Is it OK to use It?
No. An astonishing number of players use ordinary two core electric flex to connect the guitar to the amp, simply because it works and it's cheaper than regular guitar cable. Big mistake. It's a mistake because a guitar lead is nothing more than a not very efficient radio aerial connected to your extremely loud and very efficient Mega Gargantu-Monsta 500w stack. The amp does a great job of amplifying absolutely anything that comes down the wire. Your notes, taxis, next doors CB radio etc. Anything. It doesn't mind. And that's the problem. Until somebody invents an amp

that can tell the difference between your guitar solo and the local pizza delivery service, your job is to make sure the only signal to reach your amp is the one you want. The way to do this is to make sure that RF (radio frequency) and EMR (electro magnetic radiation) can't get to the conductor of your guitar cable.

The difference between a guitar cable and a piece of electric flex is easy to see. A guitar cable has one smaller central conductor surrounded by another thinner core. The outer core is the screen, connected to earth it shields the central conductor from stray frequencies. An ordinary piece of electric flex contains two conductors laid alongside each other and no screen at all. This makes it perfectly suitable for speaker wire because the speaker is a passive device (unpowered, relying on current transmitted down a wire) so it's unaffected by RF etc. Electric cable is also heavier gauge making it very suitable for the relatively high voltages that an amplifier might produce. Moreover, speakers are often placed far away from amps in places where the wire might be trodden on etc. So electric flex is OK for speakers but not for amps, geddit?

Line loss means that as your signal travels down the cable it meets a certain amount of natural resistance from the material that the cable is made from. As different cables are made from different materials the line loss varies from cable to cable.. A cable that's been used and abused for a while will also have a greater resistance than a brand new one. If you find that you need a cable that's longer than 10 metres you should seriously consider investing in an inexpensive radio system for your guitar.

Fuses, earth and other electrical safety

Guitar amps are usually earthed devices. This means that there is a good physical connection between the wire from the wall socket, into the plug, up to your amp, along your wire and into your guitar. The earth wire is there for a very good reason. The first thing to know about electricity is that it's always looking for the quickest route to earth, the ground, call it what you like. This in essence is how electrical devices work. Now if you drop your amp on the way to the gig, you might damage it in such a way that it works but live current flows through the chassis. If you then remove the earth from the plug, the live current has only one way to go – *through you.* The rule is simple.

Never under any circumstances disconnect the earth from your amp, the trailing lead or the plug in the wall.

no matter what the bright spark bass player says.

Recent legislation has put the onus on the venue to provide RCD devices wherever electricity is used on stage or in a place of entertainment. An RCD (residual current detector) looks like an ordinary domestic outlet with an additional 'trip' switch. If the RCD detects minute voltages at the earth pin of the RCD input it will assume that the equipment connected to it is faulty and will remove the power immediately. Equipment like this has already saved lives. If your amp or pedals cause the RCD to trip repeatedly you must have your equipment serviced and made safe.

Remember that you carry responsibility for your gear and if someone is hurt because you didn't take care – you could be held legally responsible.

Earth loop

Earth 'loop' noise is simply all the mains borne interference that is swimming around in the national grid. The problem is that ideally a complete audio system should be earthed at just one point. If two items of equipment have their own earth connections, and the equipment is connected together by unbalanced (hot and screen) cable then low frequency hum will be transmitted to the amp as the screen of the cable is connected to earth at both ends. The only way to cure it is to remove the screen conductor from the jack plug connected to the input of your amp. Unless your equipment is part of a managed studio rig with weighted and balanced earth connections on no account remove the earth from any item of equipment.

Fuses

Most of your equipment can be adequately protected with a 5amp fuse in the plug top. If the fuse repeatedly blows then the amp needs repairing. Most amps and other electrical devices with fragile circuitry also have additional lower rated fuses.

Which to plug in first, the guitar or the amp?

Power up your amp but don't switch on. Plug your guitar in then switch on. Saves speakers from the potentially damaging thump as you plug in your guitar and saves bugging the hell out of the rest of your band.

13

Fender and Gibson history

50's Fender Telecaster®

Between them, these two manufacturers shaped the look and feel of the guitar (and of popular music) more than any other. Gibson as a company is slightly older, Fender still comes on a bit like the new boy. The complete and very detailed history of both these companies is available elsewhere, but here's a potted history of both just to whet your appetite.

Fender Electric Instrument Company

Clarence Leo Fender (1909 – 1991) developed a keen interest in electronics from his uncle who owned an auto-electric shop in California during the 1920's. Although trained as an accountant his technical nature led him to a number of ventures, from renting his home made public address systems to baseball games, repairing radios, and even designing an automatic record changer.

Eventually Leo Fender started a small radio repair business, and in the late 1930's a man known as 'Doc' Kauffman visited Leo Fender's shop to have a musical instrument amp (possibly a Rickenbacher) repaired. Leo Fender was interested in music and invited Doc Kauffman to become his partner in a business designing and building (lap) steel guitars and amplifiers.

The Fender Esquire

Fender's first single pickup guitar called the 'Esquire' was shown at a New York trade show in 1949. This guitar was unpopular at the show for a number of reasons including the absence of a truss rod. An improved model, called the 'Broadcaster' complete with two pickups and a truss rod, was released a year later. A dispute over names with Gretsch (who had a set of Broadkaster drums) led to the renaming of the Broadcaster to the Telecaster (maintaining the communication theme) in February 1951.

The guitar was eventually a success and the Fender Telecaster® guitar has been in production ever since. Leo's radio repair man nature is evident in the simple but very effective shape and design of the Telecaster. The guitar body is shaped but not profiled to accommodate the elbow or heel. This simple design meant that the Telecaster body could be bandsawn out in a few minutes. Secondly the bolt on neck meant that one person could make the body while another made the neck, and if the neck was no good then the body could still be used.

The patented bridge is simplicity itself. One metal ashtray with three long bolts through metal bridge pieces. Although simple to us today these intonation screws were an innovation in 1950 and were advertised as a selling point alongside the bolt on neck and twin pickups.

Everything about the Telecaster points to efficiency. At the same time each part, from the individual machine heads to the stamped metal bridge, has a positive effect on the guitar. Nothing is extra, nothing is wasted. To see some flourish in Leo Fender's designs you have to wait until 1954 for the Fender Stratocaster®. With the Tele everything was tied down and functional; in contrast the Stratocaster features a long swirling headstock, big contours and even the removing of some of the wood at the sides and rear to make the guitar more comfortable to play.

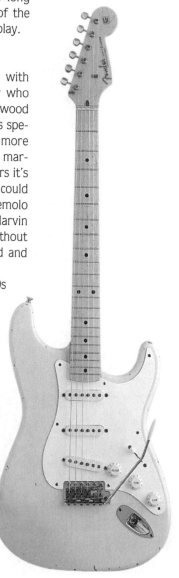

Leo's tremolo arm

The Fender tremolo was designed by Leo Fender in association with Freddie Tavares, a Hawaiian musician and orchestral guitar player who specialised in Hawaiian lap steel guitar and often performed in Hollywood movies. Freddie was first call for this kind of job and he brought this speciality to Fender to help Leo Fender develop a tremolo with much more travel than the Vibrola arms that Gibson and other companies were marketing. As Fender already had a good business making lap steel guitars it's not unreasonable to imagine Leo Fender designing a tremolo which could help the electric guitar player make the same kind of sounds. This tremolo was much more exciting and players such as Buddy Holly, Hank Marvin and Jimi Hendrix all capitalised on its advanced design. Arguably without Leo Fender and Freddie Tavares we wouldn't have the shred speed and dive-bomb players that we have today.

Leo Fender and his partners went on through the 1950's and '60s to create some of the most innovative and influential instruments the world has ever seen. In 1962 the company was bought and taken over by the CBS company, who attempted to modernise and expand the company. A parallel can easily be drawn between this and the effect that a large corporate record company might have on a young and vital independent record label. The effect was to apply overweight management and manufacturing structures onto a small successful firm which resulted in a period of fluctuating quality and design, just in time for Japanese guitar manufacturers to move into the European market.

The Fender Squier®

In the early part of the 1980's Fender responded by producing their own range of affordable Squier guitars and successfully turned the competition to their advantage. The Fender Squier Stratocaster is now one of the best selling guitars in the UK. Leo Fender died on Tuesday, March 21st 1991.

50's Fender Stratocaster®

The Gibson Guitar Co

The Gibson Guitar Co was founded by Orville Gibson in the 1800's to make hand made orchestral mandolins. Innovators as they were, the Gibson Co was fortunate enough to attract some talented engineers, in particular Lloyd Loar, who left Gibson after developing their first electric guitars in 1924 to form his own 'Vivi-Tone' company. Lloyd Loar had been chief engineer at Gibson but on his departure no-one at the company was able to follow his lead in developing the new ideas that would be vital for the future. As Gibson historian Walter Carter recounts:

Gibson ES335 Dot
(copyright and courtesy of
Gibson Guitar Corp)

'After Lloyd Loar left Gibson at the end of 1924 there was no one who filled the 'acoustical engineer' spot. Under the leadership of Gibson general manager Guy Hart, who took over in 1924 and was succeeded by McCarty in 1948, most of the design ideas came from salesmen in the field. For example, it was salesman Tom Peacock who demanded a dreadnought-size flat top to compete with the Martin D models. Consequently, the typical chain of events in the 30s would be:

1 a new idea hits the market (Rickenbacker with an electric lap steel, for example, or Epiphone's larger-body archtops), then

2 Gibson furiously brings a model to market that goes one better.'

So for nearly a quarter of a century Gibson was succeeding as a guitar manufacturing company but was relying on the competition for new ideas. Two things then happened in quick succession. Firstly Fender were becoming a big noise in California, the Broadcaster was only a few months away in 1948. Secondly, with the appointment of Ted Mcarty, Gibson finally had an engineer and innovator at the helm and could begin to design new instruments. In fact it is possible to imagine that, without Ted Mcarty, Gibson may not have survived the rush of new technology from Fender, or may have survived but with a much smaller profile perhaps along the lines of the CF Martin Co.

It wasn't long before Mcarty decided that Gibson should have a solid body guitar. However he had to be careful. Gibson had a few disappointments in the past with technically sound inventions which were not accepted by regular Gibson dealers and customers. Gibson's excellent reputation was and is based on craft and tradition. Mr Mcarty had to build this into the new electric solid body and spent some time experimenting with materials including an all maple guitar which never made it into production. The aim of these experiments was to find a combination of woods that would provide the best combination of tone and weight.

Eventually a solid bodied mahogany and maple guitar was developed with a carved top. This had the additional benefit of discouraging copyists for a while, as the carved top was expensive to produce and much more difficult to imitate. Ted Mcarty had designed most of this new model before meeting Les Paul, but Gibson still needed an established artist to endorse their new guitar. Coincidentally, a few years before these experiments a recording artist called Les Paul had approached Chicago Musical Instruments (who had bought the Gibson company in 1944) with his idea for a solid bodied instrument with two pickups. CMI had rejected his ideas, probably remembering previous experiments and not wishing to mess with an already winning brand name. However in 1952 Ted Mcarty was ready to produce his guitar and by this time Les Paul was a bona fide recording success. Like every instrument manufacturer Gibson had many endorsees, mostly from the world of jazz, and it seemingly made sense to have their new model endorsed by a young recording star. The benefit to Gibson would be that their guitar would stay within the Gibson tradition while attracting the attention of new players.

Les Paul Standard
(copyright and courtesy of
Gibson Guitar Corp)

So – and not for the first time – Gibson developed a new guitar in association with a Gibson endorsee. The new guitar would have a scale of 24 3/4 inch and 22 frets. The electronics were simple, just two single coil pickups each with tone and volume controls and the guitar featured an unusual 'trapeze' tailpiece suggested by Les Paul. Les Paul also specified the gold coloured metallic finish paint work that was to give Les Paul guitars from 1952 to 1958 the name of 'Gold Top'. Only these two features, and the Les Paul signature made it from the drawing board to the production model. Unfortunately the Les Paul 'trapeze' tailpiece wasn't a success, and it was eventually discontinued in late 1952.

Ultimately this guitar had a formula that would suit all sides. It was a true Gibson guitar with all the hand carved tradition that would reassure Gibson's existing customers and dealers. At the same time the new guitar had a a little innovation in the form of the tailpiece and a funky paint job to boot. Above all, for the dealers it was endorsed by an already accepted member of the musical establishment. So if the kids want their first Gibson, let 'em have it.

In 1955 the Les Paul Gold Top sold for $235. This put the Les Paul about midway in Gibson's catalogue above simpler models such as the Les Paul junior ($110) and Special ($169.50). Nevertheless, it wasn't plain sailing, and the Les Paul was to receive several revisions before the guitar appeared with the specifications it has today. Firstly the inconvenient Trapeze Tailpiece was replaced with a new Gibson invention the 'Tune-O-Matic', fitted firstly to the more expensive custom and finally to the standard in 1955. In 1957 Gibson added Seth Lovers PAF pickups to the Les Paul in an attempt to cut down on the noise and hum associated with single coil pickups.

The problem with single coil pickups was that they picked up hum and background noise along with the guitar string. While working for Gibson, Seth Lover developed a pickup that cancelled out hum by a process of phase reversal. Two coils are wired in series but out of phase, any hum is cancelled as two currents flow in different directions. The added advantages of increased output and a warmer sound probably weren't seen as important as the hum-cancelling system but players soon picked up on this Gibson product. Of course it was a blow for Fender too. In 1954 their Stratocaster guitar was fully packed with three pickups but the Les Paul now had four!

In 1958 the Les Paul lost its Gold Top finish and was produced with a Cherry Sunburst instead and around this time the guitar was re-named 'Les Paul Standard' by Gibson. By this time the only part of Les Paul that remained on this guitar was his signature on the headstock. Finally in 1961 the Les Paul Standard was discontinued altogether. Production wouldn't start again until 1975.

Gibson didn't know, but after forty years the Cherry Sunburst finish would age into a beautiful golden colour while the maple top underneath gradually revealed its wonderful flaming. At the same time the pickups in the guitar would mellow as the magnets decayed to produce an inimitable tone. The combination of beautiful wood, aged finish and Gibson's reputation for guitar building makes the 1958 Les Paul Standard the most coveted guitar in existence.

Fender or Gibson player?

The kind of music you play and the depth of your pocket will probably dictate your choice of guitar and your identity as a player. However the biggest influence probably comes from your favourite players. It is increasing difficult to separate musical styles and makes of instrument. Both Fender and Gibson have their own identities to players and even to non-players for whom the simple trademark profile of a Strat or Les Paul has come to be a part of the players image. The Les Paul is often seen as a blues guitar. This is partially because of the well established heritage of the Gibson company and the Les Paul itself which has a dark, rich tone with plenty of sustain for the long blues solos. On the other hand, blues guitarist Eric Clapton is a confirmed Fender player (I personally think he's a Les Paul man at heart) as was Jimi Hendrix, deeply rooted in blues music.

The Fender Hendrix Stratocaster® – left handed look, right handed player

14

Guitars from around the world

The world does not stop with Fender and Gibson. They have top billing for (almost) being first and certainly being the most successful, but that's a bit like saying the history of the car starts and stops with Ford and General Motors.

Aria

Japanese guitars made originally in the Matsumoku factory of Japan, although production is now based in Korea. Although the Aria range (from the Arai company name) started in the early 1960s, these guitars weren't picked up in the UK until the late 1970s with their very successful PE range of guitars, recently reissued.

Brian Moore.

Formed from two ex Gibson and Steinberg employees to make high quality custom guitars of non-traditional composite materials. The Brian Moore range was launched at the NAMM trade show in 1994 with their MC/1 guitar, a solid bodied guitar with a composite moulded body and premium maple top. These guitars are expensive but are a dream to play and hear. Seymour Duncan pickups and Wilkinson trem complete the spec.

Carvin

Started out as a mail order company making very high quality original design guitars, basses and amps now available in the UK through a dealership. Carvin aren't well known in the UK as being a mail order company no real volume of sales existed in the UK until a few years ago. Their guitars are very high quality with quality fittings.

Cort

Known in the UK as Tanglewood. Korean made clone guitars at various price. Fine range of acoustic and electric guitars, just branching out into the non-clone world with their Jetstream models.

Dean

Another quality US maker with a budget brand made in the Far East. Dean has a name for wild shaped solid bodied rock n' roll guitars. US made range are mid to high price point, Far Eastern models are less expensive but feature generic fittings.

Epiphone

The official name of Gibson's manufacturing operation in the Far East. These guitars are the only copies allowed to bear the Gibson name and they deserve it. Manufactured in Korea at a high price point the Epiphone range is now becoming collectible by itself with solid bodied Les Pauls, Nighthawks, Dot 335's, etc. Pretty much any Gibson guitar that's now so out of reach is available at a much more reasonable price under the Epiphone name. Quality is uniformly high, pickups and fittings typically Korean.

Fernandes

Always at the top end of the Japanese clone market – Fernandes have seemingly made a career out of taking the best of what the USA has to offer, enhancing it and selling it back at a profit. Fernandes were once just another brand of Japanese copies but after the Fender lawsuit watershed of the mid eighties their attention turned to creating high quality guitars at the sort of prices that only the Japanese and now the Koreans seem to be able to manage. By the end of the 1980's, Fernandes were making their reputation with a wide range of guitars and attracting some big name players like Steve Stevens. Rock 'n roll was obviously the way to go and that's where Fernandes are today, producing competitively priced guitars for the European and Japanese guitarist. No longer just a copyist, Fernandes are now leading with technological innovation and more big name endorsements just around the corner. If you see one under £200 it's a bargain.

Gretsch

High quality USA archtops from 1950. The Gretsch company has had a chequered career under various parent companies but recently has found new life under Gretsch family ownership. At this time Gretsch are the name for expensive big bodied semi-solid and arch top guitars such as the White Falcon, Country Gentleman and solid bodied show-offs such as the Silver Jet. Always valuable in the second hand market.

Guild

USA made line of high quality original design solid bodied guitars from 1963 to 1970. Now owned by Fender Musical Instruments, their solid bodied range never found as much success as their acoustic range recently reintroduced in the UK with their D4 jumbo acoustic in 1996. Always high quality instruments which never realise as much as they should on the second hand market.

Guild guitar logo

Hamer

Great fun, quirky and characterful guitars from a US maker. The Hamer company began making clones in 1975 but expanded to their own models in the eighties. Known especially for original solid bodied guitars and custom two, three and five neck guitars. Not wild on the second hand market but worth a look if you get the chance.

The Jackson KE1

Hohner

Brand name for guitars from a number of manufacturers in a number of Asian and European countries. Mostly clone guitars with occasional original features and fittings. Good value at resale for the right guitar.

Hofner

East – then West German family company who in the 1960s produced countless numbers of guitars for export to the UK. Most notable for models such as the President and Senator which still make good prices at resale. Hofner guitars generally weren't that well made but being cheap and much more available than US made guitars they were very successful right up to the big Japanese imports started appearing in the 70s

Ibanez

Long established Japanese manufacturer from the early 1970s. Ibanez were one of the first Japanese manufacturers offer real competition to the American market. Very wide catalogue of instruments including budget Korean range, they offer a wide range of original models from hand made George Benson and Pat Metheny guitars to the inexpensive but well made Blazer series. Always good value at resale especially for their volume selling Roadstar series. Good fittings and finish.

Jackson

Great US maker with truly original ideas especially a favourite of heavy metal and rock players. Their groundbreaking Dinky range was a turning point. Now making a wide catalogue of guitars including the obligatory Korean copies. Good resale and always a great sound.

Parker Fly

Parker are alone in creating a rarity in British guitar building – an innovative new instrument – the Fly – which breaks from the norm but manages to remain in production for more than 12 months. The secret of their sucess is that the Fly is a genuinely playable guitar in the traditional sense while managing to incorporate numerous features, piezo and magnetic pickup systems, glass fibre body, etc. The marriage of technology and tra-

The Parker Fly Deluxe features a one-piece poplar body and a basswood neck.

dition is a difficult one, especially in the small world of premium range guitar manufacture and it's for this achievement as well as their sucess in creating a brand new instrument which doesn't look like a Gibson or a Fender that they should be applauded. If there's ever been a problem with the Parker Fly it's been the price – a shade under £2000. This wasn't ever a problem for customers such as Reeves Gabriels, but the rest of us can console ourselves with the Parker Nitefly 1 which manages to incorporate most of what made the Fly so attractive without leaving our wallet out of breath.

Paul Reed Smith (PRS)

Premium range of high quality solid bodied guitars for the professional since 1985. All PRS guitars feature fine woods, extreme quality and superb finishes. If you have one already then hang on to it. The endorsement of Gibson man Ted Mcarty might mean this is the next '58 Standard at auction when all the real ones have disappeared to museums.

Peavey

Peavey make a very successful range of guitars and amps with their guitars having slightly less profile in the UK. Their most obvious endorsee is Eddie Van Halen who designed his 'Wolfgang' guitar with Peavey. Often overlooked which is such a bad decision, these guitars might be a little soul less but offer good value for money.

Rickenbacker

Adolph Rickenbacker and George Beauchamp were part of the small group of executives and entrepreneurs who were at the beginning of Orange County innovation in guitars during the 1930s and 40s. The Rickenbacker Co had an eye for design, and produced some classic instruments which found justifiable fame in the hands of The Byrds and The Beatles. The Rickenbacker 360 range remains a virtual vintage whose day in the resale market is just around the corner.

Peavey Wolfgang, as played by Eddie Van Halen

Takamine

High quality range of acoustic/electric guitars from the Japanese Sakashita factory. All Takamine guitars feature their innovative palathetic pickup system which incorporates magnetic 'pseudo-pole pieces' inside the guitar bridge similar in looks to a staggered magnetic pickup and allows for string balance. The Takamine looks as good as it sounds and is a good buy brand new or second hand.

Tanglewood

Rapidly developing distributor of instruments from the Korean Cort factory under the name of Tanglewood in the UK. Value instruments at really good prices.

Washburn

USA and Japanese made guitars depending on the model, very successful in the USA especially for their Dimebag Darrell Signature and Nuno Bettencourt guitars. Washburn make guitars in a variety of countries including Korea and Indonesia. Plenty of high profile endorsement give the Washburn some cachet in the second hand market, but watch out for variable quality of low end models.

Yamaha

Influential and competitive Japanese manufacturer or guitars, amps, keyboards, saxophones, motorbikes, etc. They seem to do everything well, including their range of medium priced guitars and especially the Pacifica models which offer amazing value for money at the price. The groundbreaking SG2000 model paved the way for Japanese domination of the industry throughout the eighties. Their budget Korean made Pacifica range offers value for money to beginners.

Tanglewood Super Six – a good buy

Development of guitar manufacturing in the Far East and Asia

Of all the guitars sold in the UK this year only a fraction will be manufactured in America, the UK or Western Europe. The vast majority of guitars sold will have been imported from large manufacturers in Korea, Taiwan, Indonesia and China. Guitar manufacturing in Japan and the Far East is a continuation of a process that began in the early 60s. Numerous small factories were producing solid bodied and semi acoustic guitars to a usually American pattern, designed for the home market.

From these small beginnings Japanese factories grew to accommodate manufacturing requests from European distributors and importers such as Kay, Grant, Columbus and Avon, who were all attracted by the relatively low production costs. Eventually large capacity factories such as Fuji and Matsumoku were producing guitars at many different levels for anyone who could afford to buy a batch of 500 or so.

There was product but no identity until in early 1981 the Matsumoku factory produced its first range of guitars to be marketed under its own

Westone

Brand name of the first low priced playable Japanese guitars, and below, the Classsic, a current model

brand name: Westone. This was a turning point for the UK player who for the first time began to notice a playable instrument with quality fittings for about a third of the price of an American guitar. The timing of this move was no accident. The period 1975 to 1985 is a recognised low point in the history of both Gibson and Fender who were both struggling under the weight of increased labour costs and massive competition. For a period of about a year the Fender factory ceased production altogether with the exception of a few custom shop instruments.

This low point enabled the Japanese to take advantage of a need for low priced playable guitars, but up until this point were not offering anything to compete directly with premium US models. This situation changed in 1976 with Yamaha's SG2000 guitar, a mahogany and maple cap solid bodied guitar with a Rosewood fingerboard and set neck through body construction. This high quality guitar instantly caught the imagination of the UK player, disenchanted with poor US standards and not yet caught up in the romance of buying a vintage instrument. With the vintage instrument market some years away a second hand Gibson Les Paul could be found for about £150! At the time a new Yamaha SG2000 offered all the sounds of an American instrument with guaranteed production standards better than nearly anyone else.

The Yamaha SG2000 was soon followed by the Aria PE and Ibanez Artist, both quality Japanese instruments. This was a turning point for the Japanese factories and high quality 'copies' – guitars closely based on Fender and Gibson models – became very popular in the UK and Europe.

Today most of the Japanese manufacturers have moved production to other countries. The Japanese Matsumoku factory responsible for Aria and Vox guitars closed in 1987 to relocate their entire production facility to South Korea. Korean and Indonesian manufacturers have taken over the role previously played by the Japanese of producing guitars for the UK and European markets under a variety of names. Guitar manufacturing is becoming more diverse with factories shipping parts in from other countries to be assembled under one name.

The Cort factory of Korea assembles famous brand name guitars including some prestigious US models from parts originating elsewhere. Bodies might be made in Indonesia and exported to Korea for assembly with a Taiwanese neck to produce a guitar called 'Korean made'. Not all models that come from Cort are made in this way. Depending on the retail price the guitar might be made to several different grades in the factory, even very high quality models requiring hand made parts and finish. The Cort factory produces Tanglewood, Washburn and Epiphone guitars amongst many others.

15

The future

We are approaching the millennium and is the guitar dying? No. Are we relegated to back rooms in pubs, clubs and bars while Mr DJ does his thing? No. Fact is in the UK alone over 200,000 people own and play a guitar. The charts have never been healthier for guitar based bands. Five years ago the feeling was that music (at least live music) was dying a death and the question was 'is Comedy the new rock 'n roll?' Now more and more people are finding the guitar is now and ever shall be, dead good fun.

Materials and design

As tonewood timber becomes increasingly scarce, manufacturers adopt and develop brand new materials such as 'Lutherite' – an entirely new carbon and plastic material developed by Ibanez over eight years for their Joe Satriani JS 10 model. Ibanez were having problems binding an unusual chrome finish to the traditional timber body of the JS10 and invented the Lutherite compound which has the double ability to accept unusual finishes while retaining the tonal characteristics of hard wood. This also enables Ibanez to offer spectacular finishes that were previously unavailable.

Like many other manufacturers Ibanez is working towards guitars made from sustainable resources. Another of their inventions is a material for bass guitars; 'Ergonite' which achieves the required weight/size ratio considered tonally important by bass players without compromising sound or requiring environmentally unfriendly hardwoods in the construction. Ibanez have found that bass players are much more open to ideas coming from new technology, the hope is that more guitar players will accept these new materials and reduce their demand for exotic and expensive hardwoods.

Computer technology has had plenty of opportunity to creep into guitar manufacture and yet no-one has produced a guitar with a TV screen or keyboard for on stage e-mail! However computer controlled production is making quality guitars available to dealers for only a few pounds. Laser technology can show every detail of a priceless guitar for manufacturers to clone. Fender are just one of the manufacturers who now offer a cloning service for musicians who are willing to pay for an exact replica of their fragile and increasingly valuable guitar.

As stage productions become more and more complex, even at a night-club level MIDI will become more important to guitarists, Aria now offer three models with Roland GR MIDI bridge factory installed. I believe that a discreet MIDI pickup will become a common option, a little like better pickups or a finely figured top. This is now an option for the MC/1 guitar in the Brian Moore catalogue.

Guitars and record production

One of the most frustrating aspects of being a professional guitar player must be answering the calls of producers to create 'just that sound'. In my career I have been asked for everything from 'waves on a seashore' through to ' the sound of a badly played guitar through a tinny transistor radio in a Spanish bordello !' Very often the producer has heard another guitarist with a particular combination of amps and effects pedals, and wants the same sound from you.

This became a commonplace occurrence in the late 1980s when sampling came in and record producers and artists stopped thinking in terms of performance and in terms of 'sounds' instead. It's impossible to carry every guitar and amp combination with you so guitarists began to fall back on multi-effects boxes which could be pre-programmed with a large selection of tones. Although multi-effects can emulate different fuzz tones or create reverb and delay effects, they cannot alter the basic nature of your guitar. A Stratocaster through a Korg AX30G multi-effects is going to sound like a Stratocaster, no matter how much distortion you use.

Players were starting to demand a multi-effect that could go further and change the actual sound of the guitar. To meet this request Roland developed the VG-8 Guitar System in 1995.

The Roland VG-8 uses a Roland computer technique called COSM (Composite Object Sound Modelling) to build from its memory any combination of guitar pickup, amp and effect that you might require. It is able to do this because the designers have pre-programmed hundreds of sound 'models'. The VG-8 is able to reconstruct these models and apply them to other models to create a sound. The VG-8 is triggered by a MIDI pickup attached to any guitar. The important thing is that it is not important how the guitar naturally sounds as the computer is simply looking for pitch information. So any guitar can trigger the sound of any other guitar and amp combination from within the computer.

This kind of technology isn't cheap. The VG-8 currently retails at around £2,000. It's very common for a band to sprinkle musical styles all over a song using samples. This might cause a problem for a live guitar player who needs to be Jimi Hendrix one bar, Joe Pass the next and Twiggy Ramirez in the next. Instruments like the VG-8 help working guitarists to be successful by delivering just what their customer (the paying artist or their management) wants.

Guitars and computers

Guitars are able to communicate with computer based sequencers if the guitar is fitted with a MIDI pickup. This device looks a little like an ordinary pickup and is fitted usually just behind the bridge pickup attached to the surface of the guitar underneath the strings. When a string vibrates the extremely sensitive MIDI pickup senses the frequency of the vibrations and converts this information from analogue to digital form. All computers use digital information to communicate and so the MIDI pickup is able to trigger other MIDI devices such as tone modules or even control technology such as sound or lighting controllers. This does not interfere with the magnetic pickups and so the guitar can still be amplified in the normal way. Once the information enters the digital domain it becomes useful to any MIDI device, just as if the information had been created by a keyboard.

Crucially, much more information is generated by the guitar. The MIDI pickup not only has to sense the constantly changing note information but pressure, and dynamics coming from each of the player's hands always working in harmony with each other. It take a time for the pickup to accurately translate all this information into a form that you and I would recognise as musical, and this inevitably leads to some guitarists complaining that MIDI pickups have timing problems.

One of the most successful ways to use a MIDI pickup is to blend the sound of another instrument just under the guitar's natural tone. For instance a Hammond organ sound underneath a close rhythm part sounds very much like an additional keyboard player 'comping' along with the guitarist. Convincing brass parts are very easy to achieve if the guitar plays a line that would usually be played by a group of horns. The key is to use the ordinary sound of the guitar to mask the slow response of the MIDI pickup.

Guitars and the Internet

Although guitars and computers rarely meet in anger there's one area where the computer can offer the guitarist something unavailable anywhere else. Thanks to the growing acceptance of the computer as domestic appliance and the installation of world wide communications links, The Internet can be one place where guitars may brush against the millennium in perfect safety.

To receive Internet services you must have one of these things.

* A home or office computer, modem and access to a phone line
* Membership of a 'Cyber Cafe' or other public access
* Membership of an institution with a computer network providing internet services.

Leave the techno gubbins to those in the know. Basically your computer must have something called 'Internet browsing software', such as Microsoft's Internet Explorer or Netscape Navigator.

The Guitar Notes web site – a great starting point – and all for the price of a phone call!

Once (ahem) 'on-line' you need to get to a search service (I use http://www.yahoo.com) and from there search for 'guitars'. A simple search like this will produce thousands of addresses, mostly for guitar shops in Montana. You need to narrow it down a little – try 'guitar manufacturers' or 'Gibson guitars'.

I would include a visit to the rather excellent 'Web Guitar Resources' site with links to almost every worthwhile guitar related page currently available on line. I won't go much further with addresses, web pages appear and disappear with all the certainty and irregularity of a close harmony boy band. The Internet won't go away though and Yahoo is always around. So Yahoo your way to guitars and learn something!

Guitars and 'non-guitar' music

Whether it is the industry reacting to public demand, or the public being led by the music press, interest in new technology has never been so low. Guitar effects are as popular as they have always been and will continue to be. New finishes and even new materials are beginning to appear but fundamentally the guitar we play today is still the same instrument that our fathers played. Some players have found this to be frustrating and in trying to break out of the mould have created a whole new area of sounds and techniques to be explored. Perhaps the most exciting aspect of this is that the experimental guitarist refuses to be bound by authenticity or homage and is free to travel to some of the darker corners of technique. The downside is that for all but a handful of cult guitar players, the double edged sword of public acceptance and peer recognition is sacrificed as the move away from 'the blues' removes the player from the recognised norm.

The effects pedal or device is always the stepping off point. Some players (The Edge) get off on the repeats from the digital delay, so much so that the boundary between playback and reproduction becomes inescapably blurred. Delay has proved inspirational for more than a few notable players. Robert Fripp created 'Frippertronics' by utilising the sound on sound capabilities of two reel-to-reel tape machines to produce never ending passages over which more can be improvised. Robert Fripp is peculiar in this area as a world class technician and composer as well as effects enthusiast. His technique is served by his effects, never the other way around.

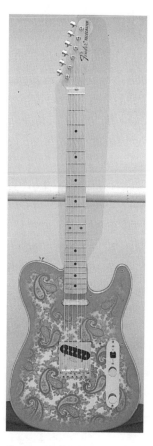

Distortion and delay in various guises all point in the same direction, that of infinite sustain. Deep in the collective consciousness that is acquired on buying your first guitar or reading your first book there lies a memory of the guitar's distant relation – the violin with its ability to create a note of never ending length and pure tone. Jimmy Page is universally famous for his attempts to bring this technique to the guitar by the use of the violin bow. The guitar however has seen s few changes since it was last used with a bow in the 17th century as the modern bridge is now flat disabling the player's ability to easily select a string for bowing.

Less well known are other devices which all have the same attribute. The Gizmo, The E Bow, the Infinite Guitar, the Floyd Rose Feedbacker, all can create notes of seemingly infinite length as if the player were using a bow after all. With digital delay came reverb and for the first time the guitarist had access to waves of blissful reverb. This water colour was successfully exploited by Robin Guthrie of the Cocteau Twins. Steve Hillage was travelling in the same direction fifteen years earlier and has recently reappeared with The Orb using his Korg A3 to produce waves and washes of sound.

The future of the guitar seems set in effects, the DSP (digital signal processor) is bound by natural law to become more powerful, and with each generation will come superior effects removing the need for the guitar player to change instruments or adapt technique. As guitars become increasingly valuable (soon to be antique) the urge to modify and customise will give way to a precious culture illustrated now by lovers of classic cars and motorbikes. Guitar fairs will be events where collectors will gather to buy screws for a resurrected 1972 Fender Stratocaster or to gaze at a particularly beautiful 1968 Paisley Telecaster, removed from it's home in a Japanese bank vault for the occasion.

The Fender Paisley Telecaster was finished with wallpaper and then lacquered!

Above all the guitar will never lose its place in the hands of the ordinary person. The guitar is the instrument of the traveller and the song-writer – simple enough to be constructed from a few natural pieces yet powerful enough to move men to tears.

16

The Internet

We reproduce here The Web Guitar Resource 'Guitar Manufacturer' listings as at the time of writing. These sites may change although searching for the company name may produce a good link. Reproduced by kind permission of the Web Guitar Resource – http://www.guitarnotes.com/guitar/WGR/.

A Basses	www.channel1.com/abass/index.htm
A & F Custom Guitars	www.fos.net/metro/
Acacia Instruments	www.essentialstrings.com/acacia.htm
Andersen Stringed Instruments	www.halcyon.com/ralevine/andersen/
Bear Creek Guitars	www.scruz.net/~bcguitar/
Bebensee Instruments	www.essentialstrings.com/bebensee.htm
Born to Rock Guitars	www.webcorp.com/btr/
Breedlove Guitars	www.teleport.com/~richm/brdlv.html
Brian Moore Custom Guitars	www.bmcguitars.com/
Carter Steel Guitars	www.steelguitar.com
Carvin Guitars	www.carvinguitars.com/
Callaham Guitars	www.visuallink.com/callaham/
Chappell Guitars	www.home.earthlink.net/~guitarsrus/
Collings Guitars	www.makemusic.com/builders/collings/
Conklin Guitar Company	www.pcs-network.com/conklin/
Cort Guitars	www.cort.com/
Crackerbox Music	www1.mhv.net/~mdegraw/cracker.htm
Dart Instruments	www.luthier.com/
Dingwall Designer Guitars	www.cyancorp.com/dingwall/
Dingwall Designer Guitars	www.teleport.com/~richm/mint.html
Eccleshall Guitars	www.thebeast.demon.co.uk/eccleshall/Welcome.html
Elrick Bass Guitars	www.upx.net/~perfitt/ebgpiccolo.html
Ernie Ball	www.callamer.com/~jeffw/
ESP Guitars	www.espguitars.com
Evergreen Mountain Instruments	www.eosc.osshe.edu/~jkraft/jnhome.htm
Fender	www.fender.com
Fichter Electric Upright Basses	www.fichterbasses.com/
Fretlight Guitar	www.optekmusic.com/
Froggy Bottom Guitars	www.samusic.com/gui-frog.htm

Gardner Guitars	www.midtown.net/~drguitar/
Gazer Guitars	www.intrlink.com/dep/gazer.htm
GGould Guitars	www.dnai.com/~ggould/
Gibson U.S.A.	www.gibson.com/
Gilchrist Mandolins and Guitars	www.makemusic.com/builders/gilchrist/
Goodall Guitars	www.samusic.com/gui-good.htm
Granata Guitars	www.nji.com/u/granata/
Gretsch	www.gretsch.com/
Grosh Guitars	www.pacificnet.net/~groshguitars/
Hamer	www.kamanmusic.com/hamer/
Jay Hargreaves	w.cybozone.com/fg/hargreaves1.html
Hembrook Custom Guitars	www.realtime.com/~rangrbob/hembrook.html
Stephen Holst Guitars	www.rio.com/~guitars/
Anthony J. Huvard	www.cybozone.com/luthier/
Ibanez Guitars	www.ibanez.com/
Ibanez Vintage Guitars	www.comcat.com/~alnico5/
Ithaca Guitar Works	www.guitarworks.com/
JB Player	www.jbplayer.com/
Steve Jarman Guitars	www.users.dircon.co.uk/~jarman/
K & S Guitar Co.	www.california.com/~kands/
Kaman	www.kamanmusic.com/
Kirk Sand Guitars	www.teleport.com/~richm/sand.html
La Si Do Guitars	www.chatsubo.com/only/lasido.html
Mark Lacey Guitars	www.laceyguitars.com
Lakewood Guitars	www.lakewoodguitars.com/
Larrivee Guitars	www.larrivee.com/
Lowden Guitars	www.samusic.com/gui-lowd.htm
Mike Lull Custom Guitars	www.halcyon.com/guitarwk/
Manne guitars home page	www.atnet.it/manne/
Manson Guitars	www.samusic.com/gui-mans.htm
Martha's Vineyard Guitar Co.	www.tiac.net/users/mvguitar/
C.F. Martin and Company	www.mguitar.com/
Metropolitan Guitars	www.io.com/~robintx/Metro/
Modulus Guitars	www.modulusguitars.com/
Monteleone Instruments	www.makemusic.com/builders/monteleone/
Nolte Guitars	www.eosc.osshe.edu/~jkraft/jnhome.htm
Olson Guitars	www.teleport.com/~richm/olson.html
Ovation Guitars	www.kamanmusic.com/ovation/
Peavey	www.peavey.com/
Paul Reed Smith Guitars	www.prsguitars.com/
Protigi	www.hiline.net/protege/
Jim Redgate Guitars	www.ozemail.com.au/~redgate/
Rhinehart Guitars	www.eurekanet.com/~rhinehart/
Robin Guitars	www.io.com/~robintx/Guitar/
Santa Cruz Guitars	www.samusic.com/gui-sant.htm
Simpson-James Guitars	www.connix.com/~sjguitar/

Sadowsky Guitars Ltd	www.sadowsky.com
Schecter Guitar Research	www.schecterguitars.com/
Seagull Guitars	www.lasido.com/
Sonam Dasara	www.carroll.com/p/sonam/
Steinberger	www.gibson.com/products/steinberger/steinberger.html
Takamine	www.kamanmusic.com/takamine/
Taylor Guitars Home Page	www.aloha.net/~rexmax/taylor/
Tobias	www.gibson.com/products/tobias/tobias.html
The TommyHawk Travel Guitar	www.gbase.com/tommyhawk/
Travis Bean Guitars	www.dsm.fordham.edu/~jodi/bean.html
Treker Custom Guitars and Basses	www.amsquare.com/guitar/treker.html
Vagabond Guitars	www.samusic.com/gui-vgbn.htm
Warr Guitars	www.deltanet.com/warr/
Warwick	www.warwickbass.com/
Washburn Guitars	www.washburn.com
Rene Wilhelmy	www.infobahnos.com/~rwil/
Wilkins Guitars	www.infi.net/~mag2/wilkins.html
Yamaha Guitars	www.yamahaguitars.com
Zeidler Guitars	www.cyboard.com/ent/zeidler.html
Zychowski Guitar	www.ibdata.com/PZGuitar/default.htm

17

Useful names and addresses

This book is the culmination of two years' research. I've spent a lot of time on the phone and in the process compiled a fairly comprehensive directory. The telephone numbers are good, so are the fax numbers. E-mail is currently a bit odd because corporate business hasn't yet got the hang of it and sole traders tend to swap ISP (Internet Service Providers) and don't tell the rest of us. If you think I've got something wrong then mail me. I am in here somewhere.:)

This directory contains some addresses from *The Guitar Magazine* 'Britbuilder' issue, reproduced here by kind permission of Michael Leonard of TGM.

Useful addresses

Arbiter (Fender, UK)
Tel 0181 202 1199
Fax 0181 202 7076

Audio Awareness, 31 -35 High Road,
Chadwell Heath, Romford, Essex,
RM6 6QN, UK.
Tel 0181 598 8081

The Audio Brothers, Unit 8,
Litchborough Ind Est, Northampton,
NN12 8JB, UK.
Tel 01327 830083

Classical Guitar Centre, 51a St Marys
Road, Bearwood, West Mids, B67
5DH, UK
Tel 0121 429 7446
Fax 0121 434 4200

Cranes Musical Instruments, 5a High
Street, Cardiff, CF1 2AW, UK.
Tel 01222 398 215
Fax 01222 667 017

Chandlers Guitars
Tel 0181 940 5874

Cliff Richard Organisation
Tel 01372 467752
Fax 01372 462352

Creative Distribution, Units 7 & 8
Anglia Way, Southwell Road, Notts,
Notts, NG18 4LP.
Tel 01623 423330
Fax 01623 420893

EMI
Tel 0181 486 4488

EMKA
Tel 0171 221 2046
Fax 0171 229 5445

Etcetera Distribution, Unit 17,
Hardmans Bus Centre, Rawtenstall,
Lancs, BB4 6HH, UK.
Tel 01706 228039
Fax 01706 222989

Exotic Guitar Company
Tel 01892 822251

FCN, Morley Road, Tonbridge, Kent
Tel 01732 366421

Fender Artist Relations
Tel 0171 602 6351
Fax 0171 603 5941

Fender Owners Club
Tel 01372 743200

Garwood In Ear Monitoring
Tel 0181 452 4635
Fax 0181 452 6974

Hanks Music Store
Tel 0171 379 1139

Harman
Tel 0181 207 5050
Fax 0181 207 4572

Hohner
Tel 01222 887333
Fax 0222 851056

Lovetone
Tel 01491571411

Macaris
Tel 0171 836 2856

Mannys Guitars USA
Tel (001) 212 819 0576

Marshall Tech Support
Tel 01792 702572

Martyn Booth Guitars, Unit 4, Old
Brickworks, Chap, Sudbury, Suffolk,
CO10 0PB.

MCPS
Tel 0181 664 4563

Musical Exchange
Tel 0121 236 7544

MCM
Tel 0171 723 7221
Music Audio Distribution, 10 Station
Parade, Willsden, London, , NW2
4NH.
Tel 0181 452 1009
Fax 0181 452 9019

Music Sales
Tel 01284 702 600

Paul Reed Smith
Tel 0171 5805544

Peavey, Great Folds Road, Oakley Hay
Ind Est, Corby, Northants, NN18 9ET,
UK.
Tel 01536 461234
Fax 01536 269029

Picato
Tel 01443 437928

Pink Floyd
Tel 0181 783 1656
Fax 0181 941 7067

Pink Floyd Music
Tel 0171 734 6892
Fax 0171 439 4613

Rean, Springfield Enterprise Park,
Northfleet, , Kent, DA11 8HB, UK.
Tel 01474 328807
Fax 01474 320285

Rhodes Music
Tel 0171 836 4656

Rocky Road Co (Mesa Boogie)
Tel 0181 450 6666

Rokas
Tel 01712402610
Fax 0171 836 3257

Roland, UK, Atlantic Close, Swansea
Enterprise P, Swansea, West
Glamorgan, SA7 9FJ.
Tel 01792 702701

Rose Morris
Tel 0171 8360991

Stewart McDonalds Guitar Shop, PO
Box 1087, Bozeman, Montana,
59715, USA.
Tel (001) 614 592 3021
Fax (001) 406 586 1030

Strings and Things, 202-210 Brighton
Road, Shoreham By Sea, West Sussex,
BN43 6RJ, UK
Tel 01273 440442

Studiomaster, Studiomaster House,
Chaul End Lane, Luton, Beds, LU4
8EZ.
Tel 01582 570621
Fax 01582 494343

Tascam
Tel 01923 819630
Fax 01923 236290

Tascam Service
Tel 01923 819699

TBC
Tel 0171 265 1567

Torque
Tel 0171 2784631

Trace Elliot
Tel 01621851851

Turnkey
Tel 0171 379 5148

Washburn
Tel 01462 482466

Woolhall Studios
Tel 01373 83067

Distributors

The following listing is by company
name followed by the distributor in
the, UK and/or USA.

The Acoustic Centre, 15 The Arches,
Livery Street, Birmingham, B3 1EU,
UK.
Tel 0121 233 1538
Fax 0121 212 4948

Active Sound, UK Ltd, 84 Queens
Road, Watford, Herts, WD2 2LA, UK.
Tel 01923 246 282
Fax 01293 246 669

Akai UK Ltd (EMI Division), Haslemere
Heathrow Est, The Parkway,
Hounslow, Middx, TW4 6NQ, UK.
Tel 0181 261 3221
Fax 0181 754 8014

Alligator Amps
Alligator, 125 Backstock Road,
Finsbury Park, London, N4 2JW, UK.
Tel 0171 226 3030
Fax 0171 226 3030

Alvarez, 1400 Ferguson Avenue, St
Louis, Missouri, MO 63133, USA.
Tel 314 727 4512
Fax 314 727-8929

Aria
Aria, UK Ltd, Unit 12 Heston Ind Est,
Church Road, Heston, Middx, TW5
0LD, UK.
Tel 0181 752 0033
Fax 0181 570 5321

Aria
Aria Co (Japan)
Tel 0081 527 113311
Fax 0081 527 113319

Arion
FCN, Morley Road, Tonbridge, Kent
Tel 01732 366421

Audio Technica, Royal London Ind Est,
Old Lane, Leeds, LS11 8AG, UK.
Tel 01132 771 441
Fax 01132 270 4836

Award Session
Radius International
Tel 01256 477222

The Bass Centre, 15 The Arches,
Livery Street, Birmingham, B3 1EU,
UK.
Tel 0121 233 1538
Fax 0121 212 4948

BC Rich
Music Audio Distribution, 10 Station
Parade, Willesden Green, London,
NW2 4NH, UK.
Tel 0181 452 1009
Fax 0181 452 9019
Blade
Blade Guitars (Switzerland)
Tel 0041 614 821802

Bow
Bow Refinishing
Tel 01689 841 967

Brandonis
Tel 0181 908 2323

Brian Moore Guitars, South Patterson
Business Park
Route 22, New York, NY, 10509,
USA.
Tel (001) 914 279 4142
Fax (001) 279 5477

Bridge Guitars
Bridge Musical Insts, The Hoplands
Business Centre, Boston Road,
Sleaford, NG34 7HZ, UK.
Tel 01529 415 372

Burns London Ltd, 21 Vernon Close,
Ottershaw, Surrey, KT16 0JD, UK.
Tel 01932 875 255
Fax 01932 873057

Button Guitars
Tel 01934 642226

Carl Martin
Danfield Music Corp
Tel 01923 237757

Carlsbro Electronics, Cross Drive,
Kirkby In Ashfield, Notts, NG17 7LD,
UK.
Tel 01623 753 902
Fax 01623 755 436

Carvin USA, 12340 World Trade
Drive, San Diego, California, CA
92128, USA.
Tel 800 854 2235
Fax 619 487 8160

Chandler Guitars USA, PO Box 4476,
Burlingame, California, CA 94011,
USA.
Tel 415 342 1490
Fax 415 342 9692

Charvel, Akai, UK Ltd, Haslemere
Heathrow Est, The Parkway,
Hounslow, Middx, TW4 6NQ, UK.
Tel 0181 261 3221
Fax 0181 754 8014

Chatsworth Guitar Co Ltd, Rain River
Studio, The Old Gables, Harrogate,
HG1 2AN, UK.
Tel 01423 536 383
Fax 01423 505 003

Clifton Guitars
Tel 0181 858 7795

Coloursound
Sola Sound
Tel 0171 836 2856

Coricidin Slides
Delta Slide Company
Tel (001) 601 378 5803

Cuenca
FCN, Morley Road, Tonbridge, Kent
Tel 01732 366421

Danelectro
John Hornby Skewes, Salem House,
Parkinson Approach, Garforth, Leeds,
LS25 2HR, UK.
Tel 0113 286 5381
Fax 0113 286 8515

Diaz
Virtual Audio
Tel 01992 613113

DiMarzio
Korg, UK
Tel 01908 857150
Fax 01908 857 199

Dod & Digitech
Arbiter
Tel 0181 202 1199

Douglas Guitars
Tel 01327 702606

Drive
FCN, Morley Road, Tonbridge, Kent
Tel 01732 366421

Eastwood Guitars
Tel 01706 874549

Eccleshall
Tel 01803 862364

Electro Harmonix
Watford Tubes
Tel 01923 893270

Electro Harmonix (USA)
New Sensor
Tel (001) 212 529 0466

EMD International, 6 Monks Close,
Dorchester, OX10 7UA, UK.

Encore
John Hornby Skewes, Salem House,
Parkinson Approach, Garforth, Leeds,
LS25 2HR, UK.
Tel 0113 286 5381
Fax 0113 286 8515

Ernie Ball
Strings and Things, 202-210 Brighton
Road, Shoreham By Sea, West Sussex,
BN43 6RJ, UK.
Tel 01273 440 442
Fax 01273 440 278
E-Mail:
strings@stringsandthings.co.uk

Feline
Tel 0181 681 3653

Fender Guitars
Arbiter Group PLC, Wilberforce Road,
London, NW9 6AX, UK.
Tel 0181 202 1199
Fax 0181 202 7076

Fender Guitars (USA)
Fender USA, 7975 N, Hayden Road,
Ste.C100, Scottsdale, Arizona, AZ
85258, USA.
Tel 602 596 9690
Fax 602 596 9948

Fernandes
FCN, Morley Road, Tonbridge, Kent
Tel 01732 366421

Fostex
SCV (Fostex), 6-24 Southgate Road,
London, N1 3JJ.
Tel 0171 923 1892
Fax 0171 241 3644

FRG
Fine Resophonic Guitars
Tel 0031 4677 8617
Fax 0031 4677 8617

Frontline
Strings and Things
Tel 01273 440442

Fylde Guitars
Hartness Road, Gwilly Industrial
Estate, Penrith, Cumbria, CA11 9BD,
UK.
Tel 01768 891 515
Fax 01768 868 998

G&L
Sound Technology
Tel 01462 480 000
Fax 01462 480 800

Gajic
Tel 0115 973 5757

Gibson USA
Tel (001) 800 444 2766
Fax (001) 615 889 5509

Gibson (UK)
Rosetti, 4 Tamdown Way, Springwood
Industrial Estate, Braintree, Essex,
CM7 2QL.
Tel 01376 550033
Fax 01376 550042

Giraffe Products Ltd, Units 2-3,
Fowler Ind Est, Bolton, Lancs, BL6
5LU, UK.
Tel 01204 690 052
Fax 01204 695 636

Godin
EMD International
Tel 01865 341597
Fax 01865 341605

Gordon Smith
Tel 0161 777 9438

Gretsch
Aria, UK Ltd, Unit 12 Heston Ind Est,
Church Road, Heston, Middx, TW5
OLD, UK.
Tel 0181 752 0033
Fax 0181 570 5321

Guild Guitars
Tel 01484 512601
Fax 01484 515384

Guyatone
John Hornby Skewes, Salem House,
Parkinson Approach, Garforth, Leeds,
LS25 2HR, UK.
Tel 0113 286 5381
Fax 0113 286 851

Haigh
Tel 01924 277930

Hiscox Cases, Millpark Ind Estate,
Hawkes Green Lane, Cannock, WS11
2KT, UK.
Tel 01543 571 420
Fax 01543 571 458

Hughes & Kettner
Korg, UK, 9 Newmarket Court,
Kingston, Milton Keynes, MK10 0AU,
UK.
Tel 01908 857150
Fax 01908 857 199

Ibanez
Headstock, Newlyn Road, Cradely
Heath, West Midlands, B64 6BE, UK.
Tel 01384 633821
Fax 01384 639186

Ibanez USA, 1726 Winchester Road
Bensalem, Penn, PA 19020.
Tel 215 638 8670
Fax 215 245 8583

Iceni
Tel 01376 583685

Jackson
Akai, UK Ltd, Haslemere Heathrow
Est, The Parkway, Hounslow, Middx,
TW4 6NQ, UK.
Tel 0181 261 3221
Fax 0181 754 801

Jaydee
Tel 0121 236 8221

Jim Dunlop
John Hornby Skewes, Salem House,
Parkinson Approach, Garforth, Leeds,
LS25 2HR, UK.
Tel 0113 286 5381
Fax 0113 286 8515

Barnes & Mullins
Tel 0171 278 4631
Fax 0171 837 6928

JJ Hucke Guitars, Tower Farm, Little
Woolford, Shipston On Stour,
Warwickshire, CV36 5NR, UK.
Tel 01608 684 887
Fax 01608 684 887

John Shelton Guitars, Unit 2, Argyle
Street Ind Est, Hull, HU3 1HD, UK.
Tel 01482 222 407

Kavanagh Custom Shop
Tel 0118 942 2559

Kendall
Tel 01235 833321

Kent Armstrong
Tel 01233 732527

KGB
Tel 0151 647 3268

KIF
Tel 01736 710608

Kinkade
Tel 01179 243 279

Klystron Amps
Ashdown Engineering, Howe Farm,
Ashdown Road, Chelsmford, Essex,
CM2 7TE, UK.
Tel 01245 477010
Fax 01245 477020
E-Mail: gooday@ashdownmusic.co.uk

Knight
Tel 01932 353131

Kustom
John Hornby Skewes, Salem House,
Parkinson Approach, Garforth, Leeds,
LS25 2HR, UK.
Tel 0113 286 5381
Fax 0113 286 8515

LA
Tel 0181 364 9726

Lakewood
Strings and Things, 202-210 Brighton
Road, Shoreham By Sea, West Sussex,
BN43 6RJ, UK.
Tel 01273 440 442
Fax 01273 440 278

Landola Guitars, PO Box 39, FIN-
68601, Pietarsaari, Finland.
Tel +358 (0)6 723 0407
Fax +358 (0)6 723 4564
E-mail: landola@multi.fi

Laney
Headstock, Newlyn Road, Cradely
Heath, West Midlands, B64 6BE, UK.
Tel 01384 633821
Fax 01384 639186

Larkin
Tel 00 353 66 39330

Levinson Blade
Tel 01404 822 011
Fax 01404 822 699
MIRep, PO Box 400, Exeter, EX5
2YP, UK.

Lindert
JP Musical Supplies
Tel 01724 782 754

Line 6
Line 6 Amps, 11260 Playa Ct, Culver
City, California, CA 90230, USA.
Tel 310 390 5373
Fax 310 390 1713

The Lowden Guitar Company, 8
Glenford Way, Newtownards, N
Ireland, BT23 4BX, UK.Tel 01247
820542
Fax 01247 820650

Marshall Amplification, Denbeigh
Road, Bletchley, Milton Keynes, MK1
1DQ, UK.
Tel 01908 375 411
Fax 01908 376 118

Martin Guitar Company, 510
Sycamore Street, Nazareth, Penn, PA
18064, USA.
Tel (001) 610 759 2837
Fax (001) 610 759 5757

Martin (UK)
Dreadnought Guitars
Tel 01903 851277

Martin Dixon
Tel 01487 823182

Matchless
Matchless Amps, 9830 Alburtis
Avenue, Santa Fe Springs, California,
CA 90670, USA.
Tel (001) 310 801 4840
Fax (001) 310 801 4828

Matchless (UK)
Tel 01392 496379

Mesa Boogie
Rocky Road Company
Tel 0181 450 6666
Fax 0181 450 8966

Rocky Road Company, Unit1
Horseshoe Close, London, NW2 7JJ,
UK.

Mimesis Pickups
Tel 01967 402144

Moon Guitars
Moon Guitars, 974 Pollockshaws
Road, Glasgow, G41 2HA, UK.
Tel 0141 632 9526
Fax 0141 632 9526

Music Man
Strings and Things, 202-210 Brighton
Road, Shoreham By Sea, West Sussex,
BN43 6RJ, UK.
Tel 01273 440 442
Fax 01273 440 278
E-mail:
strings@stringsandthings.co.uk

Musician's Union, 60-62 Clapham
Road, , London, SW9 0JJ, UK.
Tel 0171 582 5566
Fax 0171 582 9805

MXR
Strings and Things
Tel 01273 440442

Nightingale Guitars
Tel 0171 379 3572

Nobels Effects
Barnes & Mullins, 155 Grays Inn
Road, London, WC1X 8UF, UK.
Tel 0171 278 4631
Fax 0171 837 6928

Noble Guitars
Tel 0121 445 6144

Northworthy
Tel 01335 370806

Orange Musical Co 21 Denmark
Street, London WC2H 8NA
Tel 0171 240 8292
Fax 0171 240 8112
E-Mail: info@wom.net

Ovation
John Hornby Skewes, Salem House,
Parkinson Approach, Garforth, Leeds,
LS25 2HR, UK.
Tel 0113 286 5381
Fax 0113 286 8515

Palm Bay Guitars, Unit 4 Crownfield
Works, Wycombe Road, Saunderton,
Bucks, HP27 9HR, UK.
Tel 01844 347 799

Park
Marshall Amplification, Denbeigh
Road, Bletchley, Milton Keynes, MK1
1DQ, UK.
Tel 01908 375 411
Fax 01908 376 118

Parker Guitars
Korg, UK, 9 Newmarket Court,
Kingston, Milton Keynes, MK10 0AU,
UK.
Tel 01908 857150
Fax 01908 857 199

Patrick Eggle Guitars Ltd, 86a Old
Snow Hill, Birmingham, B4 6HW, UK.
Tel 0121 212 1989
Fax 0121 212 1990

Peavey
Peavey, UK, Great Folds Road, Oakley
Hay, Corby, Northants, NN18 9ET,
UK.
Tel 01536 461 234
Fax 01536 747 222

Pignose
Fairplay & Mercers Music, Unit 8
Carcroft Ind Estate, Adwick Le Street,
Doncaster, DN6 7BD, UK.
Tel 01302 724058
Fax 01302 727600

Poole Guitars
Tel 01634 220817

Pro Co
Aria
Tel 0181 572 0033

PRS
Washburn, UK
Tel 01462 482266

Raven
Tel 01582 597651
te to: , (address not collected)

Redwing
Coopers European
Tel 01902 620156

Rocktek
John Hornby Skewes, Salem House,
Parkinson Approach, Garforth, Leeds,
LS25 2HR, UK.
Tel 0113 286 5381
Fax 0113 286 8515

Roger Mayer
Mayer effects
Tel 01813304800

Roland / Boss
Roland, UK Ltd, Atlantic Close,
Swansea Enterprise Park, Swansea,
West Glamorgan, SA7 9FJ, UK.
Tel 01792 702 701
Fax 01792 310 248

Rotosound
Rotosound, Unit 3b, Morewood Close,
Sevenoaks, Kent, TN13 2HU, UK.
Tel 01732 459 838
Fax 01732 458 994

Samson
Sound Technology, Letchworth Point,
Letchworth, Herts, SG6 1ND, UK.
Tel 01462 480 000
Fax 01462 480 800

Schecter
Sound Control
Tel 0191 232 4175

Science Of Sound
House Music
Tel 0171 481 3350

Seagull Guitars
EMD International, 6 Monks Close,
Dorchester, OX10 7UA, UK.
Tel 01865 341 597
Fax 01865 341 605

Sessionette
Award Session, PO Box 3,
Basingstoke, Hants, RG24 9QA.
Tel 01256 477 222
Fax 01256 817 687

Seymour Duncan
Aria, UK Ltd, Unit 12 Heston Ind Est,
Church Road, Heston, Middx, TW5
0LD, UK.
Tel 0181 752 0033
Fax 0181 570 5321
E-Mail: Info@seymourduncan.com

Seymour Duncan (USA), 5427
Hollister Avenue, Santa Barbera,
California, 93111-2345, USA.
Tel (001) 44 805 964 9610
Fax (001) 44 805 964 9749
E-Mail: tech@seymourduncan.com

Shure
HW International, 167-171
Willoughby Lane, London, N17 0SB,
UK.
Tel 0181 808 2222
Fax 0181 808 5599

Sky Pickups
Rainbow Products, Hazeldene, Nickley
Wood Road, Shadoxhurst, Kent, TN26
1LZ, UK.
Tel 01233 732537

Spirit
Soundcraft, Cranbourne House,
Cranbourne Road, Potters Bar, Herts,
EN6 3JN, UK.
Tel 01707 668125
Fax 01707 665461

Squier
Arbiter Group PLC, Wilberforce Road,
London, NW9 6AX, UK.
Tel 0181 202 1199
Fax 0181 202 7076

Status
Trace Elliot, UK Ltd, Blackwater
Trading Est, Maldon, Essex, CM9
4GG, UK.
Tel 01621 851 851
Fax 01621 851 932

Studiomaster, Studiomaster House,
Chaul End Lane, Luton, Beds, LU4
8EZ, UK.
Tel 01582 570 370
Fax 01582 494 343

Tacoma
PO Box 400, Exeter, Devon, EX5 2YP,
UK.
Tel 01404 822011

Takamine
Korg, UK, 9 Newmarket Court,
Kingston, Milton Keynes, MK10 0AU,
UK.
Tel 01908 857150
Fax 01908 857 199

Tanglewood
EMC, Unit 6, Concorde Business
Centre, Biggin Hill, Kent, TN15 3YN,
UK.
Tel 01959 571600
Fax 01959 572267

Tascam / Teac
Teac, UK, 5 Marlin House, The
Croxley Centre, Watford, Herts, WD1
8YA, UK.
Tel 01923 819 630
Fax 01923 236 290

Taylor
Sound Technology, Letchworth Point,
Letchworth, Herts, SG6 1ND, UK.
Tel 01462 480 000
Fax 01462 480 800

Tech 21
Exclusive Distribution, Unit 10
Furmston Court, Icknield Way,
Letchworth, Herts, SG6 1UJ, UK.
Tel 01462 481148
01462 481149

Trace Elliot, UK Ltd, Blackwater
Trading Est, Maldon, Essex, CM9
4GG, UK.
Tel 01621 851 851
Fax 01621 851 932
Trajik
Tel 01243 371 328

Trantec
BBM Electronics
Tel 0181 330 3111
Fax 0181 330 3222

Vigier
Tel 033 01607 92364

Vintage
John Hornby Skewes, Salem House,
Parkinson Approach, Garforth, Leeds,
LS25 2HR, UK.
Tel 0113 286 5381
Fax 0113 286 8515

Vox
Korg, UK, 9 Newmarket Court,
Kingston, Milton Keynes, MK10 0AU,
UK.
Tel 01908 857150
Fax 01908 857199

VOX USA, 316 South Service Road
Melville, New York, NY, NY 11747-
3201, USA.
Tel (001) 516 333-9100
Fax (001) 516 333-9108

Washburn, UK, 15 Amor Way,
Letchworth, Herts, SG6 1UG, UK.
Tel 01462 482 466
Fax 01462 482 997

Way Huge effects
Rocky Road Company, Unit1
Horseshoe Close, , London, NW2 7JJ,
UK.
Tel 0181 450 6666
Fax 0181 450 8966
E-Mail: sales@v-audio.demon.co.uk

Westside (straps)
Westside, 11 Otago Lane,
Kelvinbridge, Glasgow, G12 8PH, UK.
Tel 0141 337 6833
Fax 0141 337 6834

Yairi
Ivor Mairants
Tel 0171 636 1481

Yamaha Kemble Music, UK Ltd,
Sherbourne Drive, Tilbrook, Milton
Keynes, MK7 8BL, UK.
Tel 01908 366700
Fax 01908 368 872

Zemaitis
Tel 01634 865086

Zoom
Exclusive Distribution, Unit 10
Furmston Court, Icknield Way,
Letchworth, Herts, SG6 1UJ, UK.
Tel 01462 481148
Fax 01462 481149

Music and tutor book publishers

Alfred Publishing, 7 Amber Business
Village, Tamworth, Staffs, B77 4RP,
UK.
Tel 01827 311553
Fax 01827 313 011

Bold Strummer, 20 Turkey Hill Circle,
Westport, Connecticut, 06680, USA.
Tel (001) 203 259 3201
Fax (001) 203 259 7369

IMP, Southend Road, Woodford
Green, Essex, IG8 8HN
Tel 0181 551 6139

Kevin Mayhew Ltd, Rattlesen, Bury St
Edmunds, Suffolk, IP30 0SZ, UK.
Tel 01449 737 978
01449 737 834

Music Sales, Newmarket Road, Bury
St Edmunds, Suffolk, IP33 3YB
Tel 01284 702600
Fax 01284 768301

James Pass and Co Ltd, 71 Small
Brook, Queensway, Birmingham, B5
4HX, UK.
Tel 0121 643 7623

PC Publishing, Export House, 130
Vale Road, Tonbridge, Kent TN9 1SP
Tel 01732 770893
Fax 01732 770268
email info@pc-pubs.demon.co.uk

Other useful books
Fender – The Inside Story, Forrest
White, Miller Freeman,
ISBN 0-87930-309-3

The Guitar Book, Tom Wheeler,
Macdonald, ISBN 0-354-04683-7

Guitar Electronics for Musicians,
Donald Brosnac, Amsco,
ISBN 0-7119-0232-1

Guitar Identification, A.R Duchossoir,
IMP, ISBN 0-7935-0274-8

Electronic Projects for Guitar, Penfold,
PC Publishing, ISBN 1-87077531-7

Recording the Guitar, Harris, PC
Publishing, ISBN 1-87077545-7

Music magazines

The Band (Magazine), Beauford Court,
Monmouth Street, Bath, Avon, UK
Tel 01225 442244
Fax 01225 462986

Future Music (Magazine), Beauford
Court, Monmouth Street, Bath, UK
Tel 01225 732368
Fax 01225 462986

Guitarist (Magazine), Beauford Court,
Monmouth Street, Bath, UK
Tel 01225 732368
Fax 01225 462986

Making Music Magazine, Nexus Media,
Nexus House, Swanley, Kent, BR8
8HY, UK.
Tel 01322 660 070
Fax 01322 615 636

Music Mart, 89 East Hill, Colchester,
Essex, CO1 2QN, UK.
Tel 01206 792 701
Fax 01206 871 277

The Guitar Magazine, Link House,
Dingwall Ave, Croydon CR9 2TA
Tel 0181 686 2599
Fax 0181 781 1159
email 101574.223@compuserve .com

Total Guitar (Magazine), Beauford
Court, Monmouth Street, Bath, Avon,
UK
Tel 01225 442244
email: hwylie@futurenet.co.uk

About the author

At time of writing, Richard Riley is 35 and living in Bath. Since 1992 he has written and reviewed guitars, amps, effects, recording equipment, software, hardware and diverse items of music technology equipment for guitar, computer and music technology publications including The Guitar Magazine, PC Plus, Total Guitar, The Melody Maker and Future Music. His freelancing career follows a lifetime of musical and technical associations including periods as session guitarist, record producer, live sound engineer, guitar technician... and postman. During the eighties he made intermittent appearances on TV, radio and the occasional Saturday morning TV game show where he claimed the coveted Duster Buster trophy.

He now works as a freelance reviews writer, guitar player and computer technician.

Index